PROPERTY OF
KERRY'S PLACE AUTISM SERVICES
34 BERCZY ST. AURORA, ON
(905) 713-6808

Can't Eat, Won't Eat

Please note: If you do not bring a book/DVD or other Resource Room material *back by the due date* indicated on the Due Date card:

You will not be able to take any other materials out from the Resource Room, until

1) the material is returned to KPAS or
2) the *full replacement* cost of the material is given to KPAS.

of related interest

A User Guide to the GF/CF Diet
For Autism, Asperger syndrome and AD/HD
Luke Jackson
Foreword by Marilyn Le Breton
ISBN 978 1 84310 055 3

Diet Intervention and Autism
Implementing the Gluten Free and Casein Free Diet
for Autistic Children and Adults - A Practical Guide for Parents
Marilyn Le Breton
Foreword by Rosemary Kessick
ISBN 978 1 85302 935 6

The Complete Guide to Asperger's Syndrome
Tony Attwood
ISBN 978 1 84310 495 7

Asperger Syndrome in the Family
Redefining Normal
Liane Holliday Willey
ISBN 978 1 85302 873 1

Breaking Autism's Barriers
A Father's Story
Bill Davis,
As told to Wendy Goldband Schunick
ISBN 978 1 85302 979 0

Autistic Thinking
This is the Title
Peter Vermeulin
Foreword by Francesca Happe
ISBN 978 1 85302 995 0

Asperger Syndrome, The Universe and Everything
Kenneth Hall
Forewords by Ken P. Kerr and Gill Rowley
ISBN 978 1 85302 930 1

Growing Up Severely Autistic
They Call Me Gabriel
Kate Rankin
ISBN 978 1 85302 981 5

Pretending to be Normal
Living with Asperger's Syndrome
Liane Holliday Willey
ISBN 978 1 85302 749 9

Hitchhiking Through Asperger Syndrome
Lise Pyles
Foreword by Tony Attwood
ISBN 978 1 85302 937 0

PROPERTY OF
KERRY'S PLACE AUTISM SERVICES
34 BERCZY ST. AURORA, ON
(905) 713-

Can't Eat, Won't Eat

Dietary Difficulties
and Autistic Spectrum Disorders

Brenda Legge

Jessica Kingsley Publishers
London and Philadelphia

First published in the United Kingdom in 2002
by Jessica Kingsley Publishers
116 Pentonville Road
London N1 9JB, UK
and
400 Market Street, Suite 400
Philadelphia, PA 19106, USA

www.jkp.com

Copyright © Brenda Legge 2002

The right of Brenda Legge to be identified as author of this work has been asserted by her in accordance with the Copyright, Designs and Patents Act 1988.

All rights reserved. No part of this publication may be reproduced in any material form (including photocopying or storing it in any medium by electronic means and whether or not transiently or incidentally to some other use of this publication) without the written permission of the copyright owner except in accordance with the provisions of the Copyright, Designs and Patents Act 1988 or under the terms of a licence issued by the Copyright Licensing Agency Ltd, Saffron House, 6–10 Kirby Street, London EC1N 8TS. Applications for the copyright owner's written permission to reproduce any part of this publication should be addressed to the publisher.

Warning: The doing of an unauthorised act in relation to a copyright work may result in both a civil claim for damages and criminal prosecution.

Library of Congress Cataloging in Publication Data
Legge, Brenda, 1955-
    Can't eat, wont eat : dietary difficulties and the autism spectrum / Brenda Legge.
        p. cm.
    "First published in the United Kingdom in 2001."
    Includes bibliographical references and index.
    ISBN 1-85302-974-2 (alk. paper)
        1. Autism in children--Nutritional aspects. 2. Eating disorders. I. Title.

RJ506.A9 L444 2002
618.92'8982--dc21   2001053706

British Library Cataloguing in Publication Data
A CIP catalogue record for this book is available from the British Library

ISBN 978 1 85302 974 5

Printed and bound in the United States by
Thomson-Shore, Inc.

Contents

Acknowledgements

Many thanks to:

- Harry, for providing the inspiration for this book, and not charging me for it

- my husband, Beverley, for his invaluable help and support

- Frank Dickens for his cartoon of Harry, inspired by a story by our good friend James Leavey

- my friend Sharon for her humour, enthusiasm and for nagging me to get on with it

- Babs, for Harry-sitting on many occasions

- everyone who made the time and effort to complete and return my questionnaires.

Special thanks to Brenda and Kenneth, David, Gill and Rachel, Sally and Miranda, Katharine and James, Janet and Alexander, Michele and Bradley, Deirdre and Charles, Felicity and Charlie, Lynne and David, Anna Parton and Robert, Ros Blackburn, Colin Revell, Catherine Dendy, Janet Dunn, Kathy Cranmer and Anne Farrelly.

*n memory of dearest Heather, my much
loved sister-in-law, who gave me a lot
of encouragement with this project*

I'd rather go in the cooking pot than eat any of that rubbish.

Introduction

For most of the population food is a source of comfort, pleasure and security. We actively look forward to mealtimes, promise ourselves culinary treats when the pressure is on and reward ourselves with gourmet meals out on special occasions. This is certainly my experience of food, but my son's view is somewhat different. For him food can be a source of fear, or even revulsion. This has been the case from day one and he's not alone. It's claimed that around 1 in 20 children under the age of 5 have feeding problems (Batchelor and Kerslake 1990), but statistics like this can be a little misleading if they are taken out of context. I believe it's important to look at the unique problems experienced by various subgroups. For example, feeding difficulties seem to be more prevalent in children with developmental disabilities; it's estimated that around one-third will experience this type of problem.

I've written this book for parents of children who have been placed somewhere within that hazy category known as autistic spectrum disorders (ASD). More specifically, for those who have offspring with a real fear or dislike of food, I am not talking about the fussy or faddy eater who is a little picky about food, but the child who has a real aversion to trying anything new and turns every meal into a battle with the inevitable result – Parents Nil: Stroppy Kid One.

My son is now 11 years old and was diagnosed with Asperger's syndrome (AS) several years ago. While this diagnosis wasn't a cause for celebration, his hostility towards every meal I placed before him caused me the greatest amount of anguish. Naturally, I wanted to read all I possibly could on the subject, but while there were lots of books on autism in general and Asperger's syndrome in particular, there seemed to be little on dietary problems at that time. This inspired the irrational fear that I was the only parent experiencing this particular problem, that my son was unique or, even worse, that my cooking was so awful that it had given rise to the intolerance in the first place.

Out of desperation I placed a series of notices in various specialist journals asking subscribers to contact me if their children had dietary difficulties. The response was encouraging and I mailed out more than 100 diet questionnaires to parents who were experiencing very similar problems. Initially, I had the intention of publishing a feature on the subject to help those in the same boat, but it soon became evident that I had enough material for a book. I have no special qualifications for writing a book on dietary problems, but as an insulin-dependent diabetic for more than 20 years I do have a working knowledge of the basics of nutrition. I haven't discovered a magic pill or potion to make your child eat, nor can I patent a sure-fire method that will work for everyone, but I think we can all learn from the experiences of others. At the very least there is comfort in the realisation that we aren't facing this problem alone.

1

Beyond Faddiness

Jack Sprat could eat no fat,
His wife could eat no lean,
And so between them both, you see,
They licked the platter clean.
(*circa* 1639)

It was the middle of the night and I'd been woken by the sound of my son coughing loudly. He couldn't get his breath and was panicking at the thought of being sick or choking. I dashed into his room with a cup of orange squash (one of the few drinks he'll tolerate) and held it out to him. Any other child would have taken it eagerly, but not Harry. His response was to put on the light, still coughing, and to examine the cup I'd given him. In my haste I'd chosen a cup he didn't like and his immediate reaction was to reject it, even though the contents would have relieved his symptoms in seconds. As he continued to cough, I went downstairs to select another cup with a design he could accept.

To me, this sums up the intransigent nature of the autistic child. It goes way beyond stubbornness or an unwillingness to conform. The fear of change, of accepting anything new or unfamiliar, is so great that it seems to defy all logic. When that fear is transferred onto every dish the combined talents of Delia Smith, Antony Worrall Thompson, Egon Ronay and Mrs Beeton could come up with, the fun really starts.

What does he eat?

Breakfast

- Honey Nut Loops cereal
- orange squash with calcium supplement
- mini KitKat
- mini pack Maltesers.

In an ideal world I'd prepare my son a boiled egg and a slice of whole-meal toast spread with low-fat margarine for breakfast. He'd have a glass of freshly squeezed orange juice to wash it down and maybe still have room for a healthy bowl of cereal (with reduced sugar content, of course). Reality is a little different. Every day I prepare a small glass of orange squash, the same brand each time. To this I add a measure of calcium syrup, which has the blessing of being virtually tasteless. Then I pour a minute amount of dry cereal into a bowl. With a little luck and a lot of cajoling and praise, Harry may finish the princely sum of ten individual pieces – no more.[1]

Then comes the part that really rankles. I hand over a mini pack of Maltesers and a mini KitKat – the items he really wants. Even though these are desired items, they're not automatically gobbled down. First they have to be checked for 'bits'. I'm still not sure what 'bits' are but they'll be familiar to parents of children with similar habits. They might be a slight discoloration in the shading of chicken meat, a blemish in an otherwise perfect apple, an eye in a cooked potato, a less than smooth coating on a chocolate biscuit, or a slightly charred area on a toasted muffin. Whatever their origin, they must be discarded before the serious business of eating can begin. No matter that the remaining food is cold and severely depleted, this is the way that Harry chooses to eat, and it's a pattern repeated day in, day out, year in, year out.

---

1   Since writing this Harry has progressed to eating a whole bowl of cereal (same brand), with a tiny amount of semi-skimmed milk. A big step forward.

Lunch

PACKED LUNCHES

On schooldays Harry's lunch can be prepared in record time. It's a euphemism to call it a packed lunch, in reality it's a package of snacks:

- one plastic drink container with turquoise top (the manufacturers have now changed the colour to blue but I must continue to use the old top on any new containers I buy) filled with sugar-free orange squash

- one pack of plain Hula Hoops, or for a bit of variety a pack of salt and vinegar Walkers crisps. No other flavour or brand is tolerated.

- two mini KitKats.

I dread to think what the dinner ladies, lunchtime assistants, or whatever their current job description is, think of me. To be honest, I know exactly what they think. They probably regard me as a bad mother who has no idea of the nutritional requirements of a growing child; someone who deliberately loads her offspring with sugar in the full knowledge that he'll be spending most of his formative years in a dentist's chair; an ignorant individual who wouldn't recognise a balanced meal if one hit her full in the face. I know this for a fact, because it's exactly what I would think if I were a dinner lady and didn't understand the culinary peculiarities of certain children.

In the past I tried to ingratiate myself with the lunchtime staff. I prepared sandwiches for my son in the full knowledge that they'd be returned, untouched, in their clingfilm packaging at the end of the day. I put apples and oranges in too, so they'd realise I was well versed in the arguments for providing an adequate supply of fruit for a growing child. I've even been known to slip in a carrot to appease the vegetable lobbyists. Sadly, none of these were ever eaten, but it did make me feel better.

My overriding ambition in life is to discover how to make a sandwich without bread, spread or filling, since Harry won't touch any of them. Other parents make everything sound so easy: 'Have you thought of yogurts, high-energy cereal bars, cheese-filled bagels? There are hundreds of alternatives.' Indeed there are and I'm intimately acquainted with them, because Harry's rejected them all.

On the plus side, Harry's school does allow him to eat his rather eccentric diet unchallenged, though this hasn't always been the case. Panic set in a few months ago when we received a letter informing us that sweets (and, by implication, chocolate) were no longer allowed in school lunchboxes. I had to dash off a letter explaining that if Harry wasn't allowed chocolate rations he'd simply go hungry, and could an exception please be made for him? The outcome was that biscuity type chocolates were deemed okay, but other chocolate treats, including one particular favourite, apparently weren't. Since an over-zealous dinner lady had once deprived him of the latter, we now comply with the new dictates to the letter, though for the life of me I can't see how one type of chocolate snack differs significantly from any other.

SCHOOL LUNCHES

We did give school lunches a try – for one week. The menu was excellent and offered a wide variety of foods, including cheesy potato bake, potato wedges, toad in the hole with gravy, fish and potato monster feet, roast breast of turkey, cabbage, cauliflower cheese, turkey drummers, fries, and a succulent range of desserts ranging from frozen chocolate mousse to yummy jam tarts with custard. At the end of the week we had to admit defeat. Harry went without food from Monday to Thursday because there wasn't a single item he liked. What's more he was in grave danger of becoming dehydrated because he didn't like any of the beverages on offer, including water.

However, we did strike lucky on Friday when fries made an appearance on the menu, and he polished off the lot. Sadly, the school didn't have a mechanism to allow children to eat lunch only on Fridays. We were prepared to be flexible and let him eat on any day that chips put in an appearance. After all he wasn't *that* picky. It didn't matter whether the school served up chips made from Maris Piper, King Edward's, Pentland Dell or Russet Burbank potatoes, he'd scoff the lot. However, this wasn't an option and we were relegated to packed lunches once more.

Teatime

This basic menu is a winner, so we generally serve it on Mondays, Tuesdays, Wednesdays and Fridays:

- crinkle-cut oven chips (frozen)
- one turkey dinosaur (frozen)
- tomato ketchup
- one cup of orange squash
- vanilla ice-cream or fruit for dessert.

In order to vary the meal, we have tried placing the dinosaur on the right-hand side of the plate and the fries on the left, and vice versa. However, on no account should the ketchup ever be squirted liberally over the food or it will be rejected out of hand. There is a perfectly valid reason for this – it would hide the 'bits' so Harry couldn't do his quality control job. A subtle pool of ketchup applied to the left-hand side of the plate seems to elicit the best response. This can be topped up as required.

TOP TIPS

- Do not leave the salt cellar unguarded on the table as the entire contents could be disgorged over one chip. Many autistic children seem to have an unnatural craving for salt.
- Try substituting string-like American fries for thick-cut chunky ones. With the latter, around two-thirds of the fries are discarded because of 'bits'. The thin variety seem to have fewer imperfections so there's less waste.

On Thursdays Harry is allowed a KFC or Kentucky Fried Chicken to the uninitiated. This is a time-saving treat that we can fully recommend. The staff at our local branch are so well acquainted with Harry's order, needless to say it never varies, that he only has to enter the outlet and the meal is ready and waiting on the counter.

Much to the chagrin of other customers, he sometimes gets preferential treatment: a choice of toys (everyone else gets one shoved in the box regardless), an extra chicken strip (poor boy looks as if he needs to be fattened up), a few extra fries and sometimes an adult-sized measure of diet Pepsi. On one occasion, there was a new member of staff at the counter who was unfamiliar with his requirements. Just as Harry was explaining what he wanted, a voice from the kitchens shouted, 'The usual, mate? He wants a chicken strips kid's meal, tomato ketchup and a diet Pepsi.' There are some advantages to being a regular.

Weekends

At the weekend everything remains the same apart from the midday meal. On Saturdays, I'm ashamed to admit, we allow yet another takeaway. It's invariably either a KFC or McDonald's chicken nugget meal. At the moment the latter are in favour because they give racing cars with their Happy meals, Harry's current obsession. Burger King's chicken meal was a favourite for a long time, but then they changed the recipe for fries and Harry found one too many 'bits' in his chicken dippers so they were consigned to the culinary scrapheap.

Fast food outlets could have been tailor-made for the autistic child. The peripherals – pretty packaging, free toys and informal eating arrangements – are almost as attractive as the food itself. No one is going to bat an eyelid if you request the same items over and over again, and you are actively encouraged to douse the food in as much ketchup and salt as you desire. Moreover, you don't have to do battle with those instruments of torture, a knife and fork. Finger food is easy to eat and you can make as much mess as you like.

Apart from the cost involved, I've always been reluctant to encourage Harry's penchant for fast food. It's generally viewed as an easy option and openly frowned upon by other parents. However, when your child eats so little, it's simply not practical to cut out a regular source of sustenance. To all the detractors I would say, 'Fine, but what

Can we eat when you've finished this silly pic?

do I replace it with?' On the plus side, every food has some merits, more of which later. On the minus side, each kid's meal comes with a free toy. At the current rate of two meals a week, we've had to find storage space for a total of 104 toys a year. Now that's what I call a problem!

On Sundays we eat together as a family, the one day of the week this ideal is possible. Harry tucks into a roast chicken meal and a portion of roast potatoes and occasionally he'll eat a few peas too. Aha, I hear you say, why don't you serve chicken and roast potatoes more often since this seems to be the only semi-nutritious meal he'll eat? A good point and, strangely enough, one we'd already thought of. Yes, we have served this combination on other days, but the big difference as far as Harry's concerned is that other days are not Sunday. The boy's logic is irrefutable. Chicken and roast potatoes are eaten on Sundays and therefore inappropriate on other days of the week.

By dint of the same logic, there are some things that can only be consumed in school and not at home, and vice versa. For example, chocolate mousse pudding used to be a favourite in the school lunchbox, but for some odd reason it couldn't be consumed at home. It was a school thing, you see. Similarly, cold chicken is fine for home consumption, but were I to place a cold chicken drumstick in his school lunchbox, it would come back untouched. It's a home thing, you see. I never said it would be easy.

The rest of the human race

I've got a little tired of other parents telling me that they fully understand my culinary nightmares because their Lee, Kevin or Jade is also a faddy eater. 'The poor love is disappearing before my eyes, won't touch mange tout, persimmon, pickled herrings, sauerkraut, or kumquats,' they complain. Invariably the offspring in question is built like a Sherman tank and has the culinary discretion of a malfunctioning waste disposal unit.

The parents I do listen to are the ones whose experiences are broadly similar to my own. They may have a child with Asperger's syndrome (AS), or one who has been placed vaguely on the autistic spectrum. The child may have language disorders, attention deficit disorder (ADD), attention deficit hyperactivity disorder (ADHD), various developmental problems, dyspraxia, Tourette's syndrome, or a combination of these problems. But however diverse their medical conditions, these children will all share one common factor: a very strong aversion to eating or drinking anything new or unfamiliar. In many cases, the tally of foodstuffs that are acceptable can easily be counted on one hand. Moreover, they are often tolerated only in minuscule amounts. By comparison, nouvelle cuisine portions can look positively generous.

Of course, not all children with the above disorders will have dietary problems. Many will have perfectly normal eating habits, which only serves to add to the conundrum; why won't my child eat?

Psychology versus physiology

I'm not a medic, behaviourist, psychologist, or nutritionist, but I've had to acquire smatterings of all these professions to meet the job description demanded by the employment agency that recruits mothers, more specifically, mothers of children with eating intolerances. As a layperson trying to make sense of unfathomable behaviour, it seems undeniable that a significant part of my son's problem is psychological and tied in very closely with the autistic condition. The recognised traits of obsessive behaviour, fear of anything new and a desire to control everything within the autistic's world are mirrored almost fanatically in Harry's reaction to food.

That is not to say that physical ailments aren't of consequence when children refuse to eat. Several of the families I've encountered have cited children who had difficulties in swallowing, with various food allergies, irritable bowel syndrome (IBS) and, in one case, Crohn's disease. Clearly such ailments compound the problem, but in many cases a psychological aversion to food seems to be strongly in evidence as well.

Plainly these psychological difficulties are quite distinct from the kind associated with sufferers from anorexia nervosa or bulimia, though one medic was misguided enough to suggest otherwise when my son was all of 6 years old. 'Is he making himself sick?' she demanded to know after weighing him and discovering how slight he was. Since the poor boy was terrified of being sick, I was able to assure her that he wasn't. Whether or not she believed me is another matter. I've frequently been frustrated and annoyed by the inflexibility of professionals when they come up against a condition which doesn't fit neatly into their A to Z of common ailments.

My son's problem, unlike more widely publicised eating disorders, has been in evidence virtually from day one and seems to be something quite outside his control. The decision to reject food hasn't come about through social pressures, because he's become more aware of his body and how closely it mirrors or differs from those of his peers. Controlling what he eats is not a way of coping with life's difficulties, nor is it a symptom of bad parenting or a result of being weaned on the wrong foods. The latter suggestion was helpfully put forward by a presenter on breakfast television when they had a child with remarkably similar problems to Harry on the programme.

One common factor I've noted when talking to recipients of my questionnaire is that a lot of children with dietary difficulties also seem to have extreme reactions to heat and cold. Certainly Harry will request extra clothing on warm, sunny days and shows a very strong reaction to winter chills. This extreme sensitivity was noted by Tony Attwood, (1998, p.137): 'It is as if the child has a broken internal thermostat.' Since the part of the brain known as the hypothalamus controls both body temperature and our appetite for food, is it too wild a speculation to suggest that this region might hold the answer to the riddle of why some autistic children have a marked aversion to food while others don't?

Flavour of the month

The vagaries of which foodstuffs are currently in favour with Harry and which are out, have caused us sizeable headaches over the years. Sometimes a particular food will remain popular for years, while other favourites will be cast aside after a matter of days or weeks, often for no particular reason. One sure-fire way to offend the sensibilities of an autistic child is to change the appearance or taste of a familiar product. Once a manufacturer decides to alter the packaging on a foodstuff or to 'improve' the recipe, that product becomes to all intents and purposes a completely new product and no self-respecting, paid-up member of the autistic spectrum will touch it. One solution is to keep an original cereal packet, drink bottle, or whatever, and transfer the contents from the offending new version when you're serving up food and drink. Alternatively, surreptitiously prepare the meal out of sight of your offspring and make sure that he/she never sees the packaging. However, this will only work if new packaging is the sole problem. These kids are smart and can easily spot new flavours and subtly altered recipes. Dressing new products in a familiar guise will not fool them for a nanosecond.

Manufacturers, not surprisingly, are a tad reluctant to revert to the old-style packaging if you have the temerity to point out the problem to them. One employee of a famous chocolate firm patiently listened to my complaints about new packaging on a type of biscuit Harry had formerly loved, took down my details, then kindly sent me a voucher to buy more of the stuff. I didn't like to point out that they'd missed the point since Harry wouldn't touch any of their revamped products with a bargepole, nor did he like anything else in their range. I've still got the voucher.

The need for sameness even extends to non-edibles like toothpaste. When a manufacturer changed the packaging on the one gel Harry would tolerate, I spoke to a very helpful customer services employee who wracked his brains to think of ways to help. Finally, he suggested keeping an old toothpaste tube and squeezing the new product into it. I'm still trying to perfect this technique but think it ranks alongside striking a match on a jelly in terms of practicality.

Rejection of a favourite food is something that can push even the most placid parent to breaking point. When your child eats so little, it's a major tragedy when a staple of their diet is suddenly struck off the menu. I remember feeling suicidal by the chilled foods cabinet in a major food chain when I discovered they'd changed the cardboard outer on their chicken nuggets to commemorate the 1998 World Cup.

What's more, Harry had seen the new packaging so I couldn't fool him by slipping an old outer on the pack at mealtimes. In desperation I trudged around all the local supermarkets trying to find a replacement that could be added to his severely depleted menu, only to be met with, 'I don't like the look of that', or, on the rare occasions he actually tried it, 'it's got too many bits', or 'it tastes funny'.

Eventually I gave up and Harry solved the problem himself when he stayed over at a friend's house for dinner. 'What did you eat?' I enquired casually. 'Chicken dippers, chips and ketchup,' he volunteered. Within seconds I was on the phone to the parent concerned demanding to know the name of the product he'd eaten and where she'd purchased it. I bought four packs to be on the safe side, cooked a portion and sat back to wait for the compliments. He toyed with the dippers for a while, then announced, 'I don't like them.' Through gritted teeth I asked, 'Then why did you eat them at your friend's house?' To which he answered, 'To be polite.' I suppose I have to count my blessings. My son may be incredibly stubborn and a nightmare to feed, but at least he has good manners. However, this episode did have a happy ending. To appease me, Harry agreed to try a similar product from the same manufacturer. Miraculously he liked it and it became part of his daily diet. Predictably, he's gone off it now, but I'm hopeful that it will be in vogue again one day.

The boredom factor

It's easy to spot the parents of culinarily challenged autistic children in the supermarket. They're the ones bulk buying the few items their off-spring will eat – numerous packs of identical biscuits, several multipacks of crisps (one flavour only), a fortnight's supply of chicken nuggets, several bottles of tomato ketchup, a vanload of cheese toasties and litres of one particular brand of beverage. There's a sad inevitability about it all. One day their child will go off one or more of these stalwarts and the rest of the family will be obliged to dispose of the contents of bulging store cupboards and refrigerators, or develop a taste for the stuff them-selves before the sell-by date runs out. Friends popping round for a visit will probably find themselves on the receiving end of armfuls of frozen oven chips or enough cordial to fill an olympic-size swimming pool.

Of course, there's a perfectly logical explanation for this behaviour. No matter how much an autistic child favours predictability and sameness, every child has a limit. Imagine being offered the same food, day in, day out, for not just days but possibly years. Everyone has a saturation point and the autistic child is no exception. Sometimes there's a reason other than sheer boredom when a child rejects a favourite food. It may have a subtly different taste (real or imagined), it may look different or have a different smell. When Harry contracted tonsillitis, aged 7, even his few 'okay' foods had a foreign taste, so he went on hunger strike for ten days.

As a general rule, it would appear that foods which have once been tolerated or even enjoyed by an autistic child are unlikely to be out of favour for all time. Somewhere in the complex computer that makes up our children's minds are files marked Mmm and Ugh! Foods in the Mmm file may be rejected at one stage, then reinstated maybe months or even years later. In Harry's case, toasted muffins, certain brands of chicken nuggets, cheese and tomato pizza, baked beans and mashed potato have all had a brief sojourn in the Mmm file, then found themselves unceremoniously dumped under Ugh! for no apparent reason. With the exception of mashed potato and pizza, all the other items have been welcomed back at various times and we live in hope that the rest will find favour again at some stage.

Mmm pizza…I can't imagine a time when I won't like it

2

Improvements and Setbacks

Little King Pippin he built a fine hall,
Pie-crust and pastry crust that was the wall;
The windows were made of black pudding and white,
And slated with pancakes, you ne'er saw the like.
(*circa* 1825)

The early days

The good news is that there has been some improvement in Harry's eating habits since the very early days. To an outsider such improvements might appear negligible, but they represent a significant step forward to us. From the beginning Harry had a very casual attitude to sustenance. He was placed on formula milk at a relatively early stage in proceedings, though I'd been a big advocate of natural methods prior to the birth. This earth mother attitude was soon knocked out of me when I encountered nothing but resistance at feeding times. I knew all the textbook reasons for breast feeding: a greater bond between mother and child, the building up of antibodies towards infection, the presence of active enzymes and live cells in breast milk which help a baby to thrive. And, as a bonus, he'd save his mother some hard-earned cash.

The only drawback was that nobody seemed to have explained these benefits to Harry. Faced with overwhelming opposition, I eventually gave up, shoved a bottle of Cow & Gate formula milk in his direction and castigated myself daily for being a failure as a mother. The process of rejection was one I soon got used to. In rapid succession he went off Cow & Gate milk, Oster milk and, just before his first birthday, cow's milk. He wouldn't touch soya milk and I'm afraid I laughed openly when someone suggested goat's milk as an alternative.

In compliance with the advice in my well-thumbed medical textbook, I didn't try to wean him too early. Harry was around four or five months old when he moved on to solids. I optimistically bought a blender so I could purée fresh fruit and vegetables for him and invested in a weaning recipe book, which was soon superseded by a textbook dealing with faddy eaters. I mashed, puréed, boiled and cut up tiny portions of food for him. I varied the eating utensils, provided attractive bowls decorated with his favourite characters, pretended the spoon was a train going into a tunnel, made funny faces out of mashed potato and veg, tried to create an attractive and stress-free environment for meal-times – and still he wouldn't eat.

In fairness, he did eat some things ad nauseam. We discovered a brand of rusks that found favour, one particular type of bottled babyfood that apparently tasted better than mother's homemade variety (I should like to stress that I did not become hurt and embittered because of this), the occasional pear (Conference only), tiny bites of apple (Cox's), grapes (green, seedless), Dairlylea cheese slices and teeny pots of fromage frais (with no 'bits' of course).

As time passed, we also discovered that Harry had a grudging admiration for junk food. His first visit to a fast food outlet, for a friend's party, was singularly unspectacular. He toyed with a few fries and left the remainder of the meal. However, the fact that he'd eaten something was remarkable enough to merit a return visit. Very gradually he took a single bite of a chicken nugget and, several visits later, polished off a whole one. Over a period of time, chicken nuggets and fries joined his 'okay' list of familiar foods and he even began to request them.

I was well acquainted with the need to provide a healthy diet for growing youngsters, knew the theory of the correct proportions of carbohydrates, fats and proteins to include in a meal and did my best to provide a balanced diet at home. I also subscribed to the beliefs of the You Are What You Eat Brigade and was determined to provide good, nutritious food wherever possible. However, it soon became clear that we could take this particular horse to water but we couldn't make him drink, so to speak, or, to quote Harry when he was able to articulate what he was feeling, 'It looks good and smells nice but I don't want to eat it.' When he learnt the phrase 'that's disgusting', we reached a plateau on the eating learning curve. I am still searching for a diet book that will sanction the use of an intravenous drip at mealtimes.

To compound the problem, Harry appeared to be having a number of mini fits or 'absences' in the early months of his life. Concerns that he could be epileptic led us to request an electroencephalogram (EEG) at the local hospital. The first result showed no significant abnormalities, but as he continued to experience these fits over a lengthy period we eventually requested a second test, which also proved negative. If medics had so far resisted the urge to write on my notes, 'Mother shows textbook signs of having Munchausen's Syndrome by Proxy' (where parents cause artificial disorders in their children) they must have been having grave doubts by now.

One oddity that the medical profession appeared to dismiss as pure coincidence was the fact that these fits invariably coincided with mealtimes. As I held a spoon to Harry's lips or encouraged him to try some finger food he would stiffen, hold out a hand and shake for several seconds. It wasn't until much later, when we were trying to rationalise this behaviour, that we realised it could have been a form of protest against being fed. At this age he had limited means of communication and a physical rejection of food was his only means of showing disapproval.

Although Harry's diet was extremely narrow in the early months and years, he did seem to be selecting items from each of the main food groups. At this stage he would eat bread, cereal and crackers (carbohydrate), a limited amount of cheese and meat (protein, fat) and fromage frais or ice-cream (protein, fat, carbohydrate). In fact, as a toddler, he stole a loaf of bread while my back was turned and I only discovered the theft after following a trail of crumbs to his hideout. To my delight he had taken a sizeable chunk out of the loaf, something he wouldn't dream of doing now. Today bread and cheese are completely out of

Bread? What bread?

favour and all attempts to reinstate them onto his menu have failed. However, there does seem to be a logical reason for his rejection of bread. Harry was sick once after eating it and the association has always stayed with him. AS children may have poor short-term memories but, regrettably, the long-term memory often compensates for this, reproducing unpleasant events with photo-like clarity.

At this stage, we were desperately clutching at straws to understand our son's food fads and at one point were convinced we'd cracked it. To the casual observer it might have seemed a coincidence that all his favourite foods began with the letters 'ch' - cheese triangles, cheese biscuits, chips, chocolate, chipolatas, chicken - but we saw a deeper significance in it. Surely this was the ideal opportunity to introduce him to cherries, cheesecake, choux buns, chappatis, chick peas, chutney, chilli con carne and chorizo sausages. Unfortunately, he later added jelly, baked beans, apples and muffins to his limited menu which completely messed up our theory. Back to the drawing board!

The present

Although Harry still has a very restricted diet, we have chalked up a number of successes over the years. Some improvements have simply just happened and can't be attributed to anything we have done. Others have been won the hard way through a series of strategies (see below) of which bribery seems to have been the most successful. The foods Harry won't touch still run into hundreds, but gradually the few he will tolerate have increased.

One peculiarity we have noted is that if a new food comes into vogue, one of the old favourites will fall by the wayside. It's as though he only has room in his 'internal menu' for a limited number of items and, once this reaches capacity, something has to go.

Harry's basic likes and dislikes have changed little over time, but he has shown a willingness to try more foods within his favourite categories. For example, potatoes and chicken have always found favour but now he will experiment with these foodstuffs in various guises – chicken curry and rice, chicken nuggets, roast chicken and even cold chicken are all currently in favour, as are roast potatoes, boiled potatoes and most types of French fries. Fruit too is enjoying a revival. Harry currently likes segments of orange, pieces of pear (William and Conference), slices of apple and green seedless grapes. So far I have not been able to tempt him to try this combination in a fruit salad, but that will be the next step. Unfortunately, I am still unable to pack fruit in his school lunchbox. Lunchtime staff haven't the time to peel and pare fruit and if I pack, for example, apple slices in a storage container with lemon juice to keep them fresh, the subtly different taste is enough to render them inedible.

As Harry becomes more aware of diet and nutrition we are also able to reason with him, up to a point – a luxury denied us a few years ago. He may even try a morsel of a new product, providing he doesn't find the look or smell totally repulsive. If he doesn't like the feel of it in his mouth, it certainly won't be swallowed. This willingness at least to try new things is a relatively new development. Curiously, watching other people eat has become something of a spectator sport for Harry. He derives great pleasure from seeing people enjoy their food, though he is very rarely tempted to taste it himself. One of his favourite programmes is 'Ready, Steady, Cook', but I no longer ask whether I should try out the recipe because the answer is invariably no. I have a sneaking suspicion that the colours associated with the teams are the biggest draw. Harry's favourite colour is red and he always supports the red tomato team.

Although some progress has been made with Harry's eating habits, there have been reversals along the way – the most significant being a heightened sensitivity to noise, which seems to have become more pronounced over the years. If anyone has the temerity or misfortune to sneeze or cough while he is enjoying a meal, he may reject the food completely. We quickly learnt that the only possible response to 'Did you just sneeze, cough, or (ultimate sin) burp?' is incredulous denial. 'Me? Of course not.' If we're believed, eating is resumed. If not, the food may well end up in the bin. Similarly, if there is a fragment of food or speck of dirt on the tablecloth or his tablemat, he cannot eat until it has been removed. Since we have no control over eating arrangements at school, and since most schoolchildren have a morbid fascination with making rude noises and creating a mess, we are no longer surprised when we discover an unopened bag of crisps or an untouched bar of chocolate in Harry's lunchbox.

The future

There's a school of thought that says children will magically grow out of their food fads and be following a normal diet when they attain a certain age. When I've asked for clarification of this theory, the ages of 12, teens and, even more nebulous, adulthood have been put forward. Bryant-Waugh and Lask (1999, pp.175-6) place fussy eaters into various categories, of which selective eating seems to be closest to my son's problem. However, he hadn't the courtesy to fall neatly into any one category and could equally have been placed under the headings of restrictive eating or even food phobia. I was heartened to learn: 'Fortunately the outlook for selective eaters is really very good. Almost all such young people seem to grow out of the problems during their teenage years, if not earlier. A very small minority, probably fewer than 1 per cent, continue to be selective eaters into adult life.' Then my hopes were dashed further on in the same chapter: 'One of us … was giving a lecture on selective eating many years ago and stated that *all* selective eaters grew out of it before adulthood. After the lecture a 27-year-old man … told the speaker he was wrong. The man concerned had been a life-long selective eater (cheese crackers, Marmite sandwiches, French fries, potato crisps, spam and baked beans.).' I too have heard of adults who remain stubbornly conservative in their eating patterns, resisting all efforts to change ingrained habits. In the most extreme case, one man ate in the same café every day, always ordered the same meal, and even demanded a certain number of peas to accompany it.

In support of the supposed transient nature of this disorder, one TV medic confidently announced that children of Harry's ilk would simply grow out of their food aversions. I would like to have challenged him on this point. Do autistic children grow out of their obsessive tendencies, their social gaucheness, their problems with language and creativity? I'm confident that there is room for improvement in all these areas, but less convinced that eating difficulties will magically disappear overnight. Tony Attwood also touches on food sensitivity in his book on Asperger's syndrome:

> Some mothers report that the child was extremely fussy in their choice of food as an infant or during their pre-school years... Fortunately, most children with Asperger's Syndrome who have this type of sensitivity eventually grow out of it...It is important to avoid programmes of force feeding or starvation to encourage a more varied diet. The child has an increased sensitivity to certain types of food. It is not a simple behaviour problem where the child is being deliberately defiant (Attwood 1998, pp.135–6)

Tony Attwood believes that this sensitivity will become less pronounced with time but acknowledges that apprehension about eating and a reluctance to try new foods may persist. He advises a softly, softly approach to the problem, encouraging the child simply to lick or taste small amounts of food without the pressure of having to chew or swallow them. Although he remains generally optimistic about the long-term prospects of these children, he also sounds a cautionary note: 'some adults with Asperger's Syndrome continue to have a very restricted diet consisting of the same essential ingredients, cooked and presented in the same way, throughout their lives.'

It worked for us

I'm not naive enough to believe that there's one strategy or tip that will be universally successful in encouraging our children to eat. It's commonly reported that children on the autistic spectrum are unique characters who seem, on the surface, to exhibit few common characteristics. However, I believe there are enough shared traits to make it worthwhile to try out ideas which have worked for others (Chapters 6 and 7).

Harry's school gave us our first major breakthrough on the food front. Staff used a laminated timetable to enable him to make sense of the school day as he had a tendency to forget things. Having his lessons and daily instructions displayed on a wipe-clean board fixed to the inside of his desk helped him enormously. We decided to adapt the idea to increase his intake of different foods.

Harry's Menu

Today is

This is what I am going to eat

Breakfast

Dinner

Tea

My favourite drinks are:

Today I am going to try:

Harry's menu encouraged him to try new foods

Luckily, Harry has always been a good reader and had no difficulty following written instructions. However, the school also used a series of Makaton symbols to reinforce the messages, so we followed suit with a series of simple illustrations when we draw up a laminated menu for him. Every day we wrote up a menu for breakfast, dinner and tea with a wipe-off marker pen. Invariably the menu would change little from day

*Food pyramids and stickers from LDA are useful for rewarding mealtime successes (see
    'Useful Addresses')*

to day, but at the bottom was the pertinent bit headed 'Today I am going to try' followed by a single item: for example, fish, pizza, cake, banana, ginger biscuit. We discovered that Harry's love of structure and routine made it very difficult for him to ignore a written instruction. Verbal instructions were a different matter, his natural inclination being to do the opposite of whatever you told him, but once something was down in black and white he was more inclined to go along with it.

Admittedly, this would have had limited success without an additional carrot, if you'll pardon the pun. Each time Harry tried a new food, he got a sticker. We discovered a handy range of stickers depicting ice-cream, burgers, cakes, fries and cups of beverage that proved to be a favourite. Another version featured a range of different fruits which played a big part in encouraging Harry to try the real thing. Once he had amassed a certain number, he was eligible for a treat. In the early days, 5 stickers equalled a comic or small toy, 10 would merit a book he particularly wanted; and 25 or more a video. Naturally, we couldn't fix 25 stickers on his chart or the whole thing would have been obliterated, so we devised a system where he received a sticker for one point, then a series of ticks until he reached the next sticker target, five, then more ticks until he reached ten, and so on. The stickers were the sort that peeled off and so could be re-used again and again.

Bearing in mind that most foodstuffs were repellent to Harry, we didn't set him impossible goals. He could gain points by trying, for example, a slice of pear, even though he had tried it before. Our logic was that the more he tried one particular item, the more likely it was to be accepted as one of his 'okay' foods with the ultimate aim to incorporate it as one of the regulars on his diet sheet. He also gained points for simply tasting something, which took away the terror of having to swallow a new food. However, he could take advantage of our leniency. On one occasion he licked a finger after washing his hands in coconut-scented soap and demanded to know, 'Does that count as a point?'

Because it took considerably more nerve to try a completely new food, we awarded additional points for this feat and made sure we praised him accordingly. As the idea took off, we had to draw up a larger chart to accommodate the new foods and extra points. Eventually we dispensed with the menu altogether in favour of a permanent reminder of all the new foods he'd tried and intended to try. The new chart was simply a sheet of A4 paper with his goal at the top in bold type, for example, a visit to the Autosport show at the National Exhibition Centre, Formula 1 yearbook or computer software, and the points required for success. We divided the page in half and listed foodstuffs he had tried in one column and the points awarded alongside. These were totted up at the bottom of each page. At one time, Harry's overriding aim was to go either to Brands Hatch or Silverstone to watch a touring cars or Formula 1 race. As the stakes for this were high, he surpassed himself in trying new foods to bump up the points. During this period, scrambled eggs, toast, bananas, fish in batter and curry were added to his repertoire, though some of them disappeared for good once he reached his target. We were concerned that once Harry had achieved his ultimate goal, the points scheme would lose momentum. However, relatively modest treats such as a visit to a Little Chef outlet have since proved sufficiently enticing to keep him motivated.

Blind tastings

Many autistic children seem to have been blessed, or cursed, with heightened senses – if a foodstuff doesn't look, smell, taste, feel or even sound right they are unlikely to try it. So when a Canadian friend suggested 'blind tasting' as a way of getting Harry to try foods, we were originally very sceptical. She devised a game where her daughter sat on one stool and Harry sat on a stool facing her. First the girl closed her eyes and Harry had to feed her a single grape. Then Harry had to close his eyes while the exercise was tried out on him. To our amazement, he not only accepted the grape but chewed and swallowed it. One possible explanation for this success was that by effectively shutting down one of his senses, Harry was freed from the ritual of checking the food for 'bits' and was happier to accept it. However, the food wasn't a complete unknown since he had started the exercise and knew exactly what was on offer. When we tried to introduce new foods that he hadn't seen, he was much less willing to take part.

Transport games

Another modest success was achieved through Harry's need to conform and follow rules and regulations. My husband devised a simple board game involving trains, one of Harry's favourite modes of transport, which included the usual instructions to go some paces forward, or back when you landed on a particular square. However, he also had to select one of a series of cards depending on where the dice fell. Some included silly instructions such as 'tickle the cat' or 'hop on one leg', while others required Harry to 'eat a slice of apple', 'eat two segments of orange' or 'finish a quarter of a banana'. Because the instructions were written down, Harry took the whole thing very seriously and felt compelled to carry out the orders to the letter. At one point he looked worried because the card demanded that he should 'eat a whole pear'. To take the pressure off we said, 'Don't worry about it if it's too difficult, just try

Do you think Matt Neal would let me do a test drive?

a slice.' But Harry was quite determined. 'No, it says it here, so I have to do it.'

Originally, Harry had made up his own game with a series of squares of paper bearing names of stations on one of his favourite routes. These were bent in half so they would stand up and placed all over the house and up the stairs in the correct order of travel. It was a simple matter to adapt the first game to tie in with this one. Harry had to select a folded card from a box and follow the instructions to reach the end of the line, for example, 'proceed to Victoria', 'miss a turn' or 'eat a grape and go to Carshalton Beeches'. Nowadays his main obsession is with Formula 1, so we could easily modify the rules to tie in with racing tracks around the world.

Working with obsessions

Many people believe that it's not a good idea to encourage your autistic child's obsessive interests. However, when you've exhausted every other avenue to get them to eat, I think it's fully justifiable to home in on something that's so intensely personal to them. We've blatantly exploited Harry's past and present interests – starting with a fascination with *Thomas the Tank Engine* characters, progressing to an encyclopaedic knowledge of tube, tram, bus and rail routes, and culminating in his current interest in everything to do with touring cars and Formula 1 drivers, cars and circuits. If the promise of a new toy car, a journey on a train, or a book on his favourite subject is the catalyst that will get him to eat, then we'll shamelessly pay homage to Harry's current obsession.

Disguise it

This is a very obvious tip but one which seems to work. Harry adores tomato ketchup but is unhappy if we apply it to any food he is eating. However, as long as he is in charge of the process he is quite happy to douse dubious items with a comforting red puddle. Even though he knows what is underneath this mess, he will generally consume the whole thing. For example, he won't usually eat peas or baked beans in their natural state, but if they are hidden by ketchup they are deemed to be okay. This appears to work because:

- He can no longer see the offending food. Colour seems to play the largest part in the examples given – he's not keen on green or orange. The problem of 'bits' is secondary here as neither beans nor peas are likely to have many imperfections.

- The taste of the beans, peas, etc. is disguised by a food he does like so they are no longer threatening.

- The texture and smell of the offending food is disguised by something he really likes. Moreover, it's red, his favourite colour.

Imagine our horror when we discovered that the makers of a famous brand of ketchup were planning to introduce a green version in order to make it more attractive to children. Apparently they had done tests with a blue product before settling on deep green. In their defence, the red version will still be available. One thing is for sure, there can't have been any autistic kids on the testing panel.

Five, four, three, two, one

I don't know if my son is unique but he appears to have been born with no sense of urgency. He tends to meander through the day and gets distracted by any number of things along the way. Mealtimes are most successful if distractions are kept to an absolute minimum: no television, no comics or books in sight and preferably no toys (with the exception of fast food meals) to divert him from the serious business of eating.

One tried and tested method of keeping his attention is to set a timer to, say, two minutes while he starts to eat. If he's eaten a reasonable amount before the timer sounds, he gets a point added to his chart. If he fails to meet the target, the points are withheld but he gets another chance the next day. Many parents use this simple device for a variety of goals and it seems to be very successful.

Dogged determination

When a faddy eater initially rejects an item of food or drink, the natural inclination is to take it away so it won't offend any more. However, the long-term implications of doing this are that the child will be left with an impossibly narrow range of acceptable items, whereas if you are determined to keep presenting something over and over again, you might find that your subject gives in before you do.

In Chapter 1, I pointed out that Harry would only accept juice in one particular container for school. When the manufacturer changed the familiar turquoise top to dark blue, Harry doggedly refused to drink from the new version. For months we played along with his preference, discarding the new top and superimposing the old one on the new container. However, over time the old top became worn and impossible to clean properly, so we finally had to get rid of it. Harry refused point-blank to drink from the new version but, since there was no alternative, I decided to keep a mini chart to record how much juice, if any, he would accept via the new top.

During the first week of the experiment, the juice bottle was returned exactly as I'd packed it in his lunchbox – full to the brim. By week two Harry was away from school because of a respiratory infection, so the experiment had to be halted. In week three he tried minuscule amounts of drink – so small that at first it looked as though he hadn't drunk anything at all. Week four looked more promising. His resistance was clearly wearing a bit thin because by Thursday he'd consumed half the contents, but we suffered a setback on Friday when only one-third of the juice had been drunk. However, there was a simple explanation for this. The straw had become detached from the lid, and he couldn't have drunk any more if he'd wanted to. I continued to chart the results over a period of nine weeks and, though the general trend was encouraging, there were several dips and reversals along the way. However, by the middle of the final week I unpacked a completely drained juice bottle (and it hadn't sprung a leak). Success!

Food is fantastic

When the chips were down, we sometimes resorted to unconventional methods. At one stage my husband decided that hypnosis was worth a try and would tell a half-asleep Harry that he loved chips and chicken (true), but was particularly fond of baked beans (at the time, false). After several weeks of this treatment, Harry did try baked beans and in fact they became a favourite for about three months. We still don't know if this subliminal approach really worked, or if he was desperate to shut up his dad so he could get a decent night's kip.

3

I Blame the Parents

Pat-a-cake, pat-a-cake, baker's man,
Bake me a cake as fast as you can;
Pat it and prick it, and mark it with B,
Put it in the oven for baby and me.
(*circa* 1698)

Guilt is a pretty futile emotion, but it's one that every parent has experienced. When your child won't eat, these feelings can go off into the stratosphere. It's all too easy to torture ourselves with questions that can't be answered. Why won't Eric eat? Is it something I've done? Is it something I haven't done? Did my prenatal cravings for soused herrings and pickled onions marinated in chocolate sauce make his taste buds go on strike?

In reality, it's a pointless exercise to look for someone or something to blame. If we could press the rewind button and start the whole weaning process again in near-clinical conditions, it's a virtual certainty that the outcome would be exactly the same. It's a harsh fact that in the lottery of life some children are born with good appetites and a healthy disregard for their surroundings, while others come into the world with heightened awareness, over-developed sensory equipment and the uncanny perception that any meal served in a hospital setting must be suspicious.

He'll eat anything

Some lucky parents have naturally compliant children. They eat whatever is put in front of them, try new foods without hesitation, use a knife and fork at the appropriate age and don't throw a wobbly when manufacturers introduce a 'new improved' version of their favourite food.

These parents smile in a self-congratulatory way when people compliment them on their offspring's good appetite and invariably reply that Maurice, Lotty or Tim 'has always been a good eater'. The mother of such paragons has achieved a first at the University of Breast Feeding, progressed to a MA in weaning, then gained a doctorate in five hundred ways to make Brussels sprouts more appetising, with the minimum of effort. Moreover, she is generous with her time and advice, implying that if you were to bring your fussy eater round for lunch she would have him finishing a three-course meal in no time. This textbook family contrasts sharply with the household ruled by a child with eating intolerances. The parents are wracked with guilt because David, Paula or Terry has rejected yet another cordon bleu meal in favour of a packet of crisps with added colourings, monosodium glutamate and a generous dose of salt. Clearly the fault lies with them.

The official line is that parental blame is no longer in vogue and parents are considered to be the experts in diagnosing and dealing with their child's eating problems. However, in practice a child who won't eat is an anomaly and it's all too easy to apportion blame, usually where it's least warranted. It doesn't help when experts on dietary problems express the view that 'faddy children are *made* not born' (Pearce 1991, p.27). This author goes on to suggest: 'Most of the food fads that children have are picked up from the attitude or example of other people. Food fads are rarely due to deep inborn dislikes that are present from birth and which never change for the rest of time. The fads are most frequently due to social customs and habits.' Even the terminology used to describe childhood eating problems may have negative connotations. The phrase failure to thrive (FTT) is typically used to describe poor nutrition in youngsters aged up to three. Some professionals are reluctant to use the term as 'it implies either a disease process or a mixture of social causes, often incompletely understood and implying blame of the parents' (Kessler and Dawson 1999, p.xv). However, we're not let off the hook if others aren't blaming us, because we're pretty darn good at doing it ourselves. The irony is that no matter what tactics have been employed to get our children to eat, someone somewhere will be only too happy to tell us that we've got it all wrong and have made crucial mistakes at various key stages in our child's upbringing. And if the rest of the world doesn't put the blame squarely on the parents' shoulders, you can rest assured that granny will.

Breast feeding

When David rejected breast milk, his mother was convinced the fault was hers. All the textbooks clearly stated that any tension or anxiety on the part of the mother would be transmitted to the child, thereby exacerbating the problem. The fact that she had been neither tense nor anxious before he refused to latch on was immaterial. Experts aren't interested in the chicken and egg perspective: 'Babies...can be difficult to feed, but parents may also be the cause of some of the problems...It is possible for parents to try too hard to get the feeding right, with the result that meals become times for tension and stress' (Pearce 1991, p.23). On the other hand, if we don't try hard enough, we're also in the firing line. It's widely assumed that parents who are too laid-back or who appear to show a lack of concern about feeding difficulties will only serve to make matters worse.

When David perfected projectile vomiting, in a northerly direction, at the age of one month, mum made the erroneous assumption that he couldn't tolerate his formula milk and promptly changed it, which was apparently inadvisable:

> 'Infants' relationships with the world are mediated through their mouths. Although differences in...taste and texture of foods may seem slight to us, they are major and upsetting changes to infants. Changes may include switching formulas or nipples abruptly...and introducing solid foods too early. (Kessler and Dawson 1999, p.131)

Harry and his dad, in the days when a dummy was one of the few things he'd put in his mouth.

On the other hand, if changes hadn't been made, the chances are you'd have a severely malnourished and possibly dehydrated baby on your hands. Technically, this is what's known as a 'no-win' situation.

Weaning

There is a lot of confusion concerning the best age to introduce solid foods, but it's a pretty safe bet that most of us have started the process too early or too late to satisfy the purists. The general view seems to be that solid foods should only be introduced when a child's teeth are through, at around six months, whereas semi-solids can be tolerated at around three to four months. I erred on the side of caution and didn't begin weaning Harry until he was around four months old. Needless to say, all his friends who were weaned at the three-month stage, now considered to be too early, have gone on to eat anything and everything, confounding the critics once more: 'There has been some suggestion that early weaning is linked with later food intolerance, especially to wheat products such as bread, rusks and biscuits' (Pearce 1991, p.16).

However, it's no good patting yourself on the back if you started weaning at a later stage because that too may cause problems. Apparently late weaning, due to protracted breast feeding, has been linked to malnutrition in some cases. There's also believed to be an optimum age for introducing new textures, around the age of seven to ten months. Apparently, if we miss this cue our children will be less willing to experiment with different textures in later life. Moreover, having completely miscalculated the correct time to start weaning, the poor parent is not even given the credit for recognising the problem in the first place. One authority on the subject states that the family GP is likely to be the first one to spot the disorder. The parents, presumably, having been unaware of it up to this point.

The reason for this lack of awareness becomes apparent when we look at some of the questions commonly asked about 'caregiver competence' by professionals. Listed among concerns about 'maladaptive nutrition beliefs' and possible 'mental disorders' on the part of parents that might interfere with the ability to prepare meals, or feed them to their offspring is the query: 'Does the parent have the intellectual ability to understand behavioural and nutritional recommendations?' (Kedesdy and Budd 1998, p.21). So, having failed miserably in all the other crucial areas of competence, we have the final humiliation of being designated 'thick' by some expert who has just been introduced to our child, and probably knows considerably less about their reluctance to eat than we do. At this point, we might be excused for feeling a tad depressed about the whole situation, but that wouldn't be wise. Parental depression, as we all know, is easily picked up by the child and may add to feeding problems: 'A baby or child who has a depressed, otherwise disturbed, or disinterested mother...can become depressed and apathetic and eventually...may fail to thrive' (Stanway 1983, p.219).

Toddlerhood and beyond

As the child grows, or not, as the case may be, the potential for the development of a full blown guilt complex increases. If initial attempts to get our children to eat have failed, we're obliged to get advice from a variety of experts. Doctors, dieticians, child psychologists and occupational therapists will be consulted, copious notes made and a variety of interventions suggested, which may or may not be successful:

> The child frequently arrives at the physician's office with a long list of failed interventions, including interventions devised by the parents, interventions recommended by friends or relatives, and interventions recommended by other professionals. Parents may be – secretly or openly – convinced that 'nothing will work'. (Kedesdy and Budd 1998, p.64)

It would be refreshing if experts might entertain the possibility that our pessimism could be justified. The majority of us don't suffer from a lack of motivation when it comes to helping our children. Rather it's the case, as noted above, that we've tried numerous remedies, jumped through proverbial hoops, bent backwards, got the T-shirt, and still have to admit that we don't have a foolproof blueprint to make our child eat. The expert, on the other hand, may have no practical experience of working with anyone on the autistic spectrum, but expects us to be impressed when he thinks of a remedy, doubles it, divides it by two and comes up with the strategy we first thought of, which has failed miserably.

One recurrent theme in literature on dietary problems is that things can only improve when the parents have changed their behaviour in some way. There seems to be a general reluctance to admit that the problem may exist in the child per se; rather, it is the parents or carers who are failing to carry out various recommendations. Indeed, we may come up with 'a seemingly endless list of reasons and excuses for being unable to follow treatment recommendations...Cases such as these can stir up frustration, anger, and a sense of desperate urgency even in normally calm and controlled professional staff' (Kessler and Dawson 1999, p.396).

I would suggest that such reactions are mild when compared to those stirred up in the parents who have religiously followed all instructions to the letter, but are still confronted by a child who won't eat. The prevailing assumption seems to be that if a treatment hasn't worked, it either hasn't been carried out at all or hasn't been conducted properly. Any suggestion that the treatment itself may be flawed or inadequate seems tantamount to blasphemy.

Indeed, it's arguable that more time is spent on finding the right terminology to describe various eating disorders than on devising methods to correct them. Those currently in vogue include: food avoidance emotional disorder, paediatric undernutrition, restrictive eating, failure to thrive, selective eating, food phobia, or simply faddy, fussy or picky eaters. I'm tempted to add my own contribution to this list. How about a this-child-will-not-eat-and-is-a-pain-in-the-posterior category for children on the autistic spectrum?

What works, what won't

The parents of children with eating intolerances could be forgiven for thinking that whatever they do will be interpreted in a negative fashion.

In the following resumé of tried and tested behavioural techniques there's a rider to show why some expert or other might disapprove of it.

Offering a reward for trying new foods

We've all tried bribery to encourage our children to eat. If we're really desperate, the stakes can increase dramatically in direct proportion to the resistance encountered. In Harry's case the offer of a packet of wax crayons has been superseded by a sticker book, which in turn was upgraded to a visit to a theme park. We halted negotiations long before he upped the odds to a week-long adventure holiday timed to coincide with the Monaco Grand Prix.

EXPERT VIEW

It is wrong to offer bribes in order to encourage a child to eat. This puts across the message that the food is so intrinsically awful that no individual of sound mind would even consider eating it unless they were offered a substantial reward to do so.

Offering preferred food for eating something new

Food bargaining, that is keeping back something the child really likes until she has tried a morsel of something she is iffy about or really detests, is another commonly used device to encourage picky eaters to try new foods.

EXPERT VIEW

Never play off one food against another. There are no good or bad foods; all sustenance should be given the same weight. In practice, trying to persuade your child that prunes in custard are as delicious as a portion of Kentucky fried chicken with its unique blend of eleven herbs and spices might take a bit of skilful negotiation.

Game playing with food

This typically revolves around variations on a simple theme. A spoon bearing cereal, porridge or whatever is magically transformed into an aeroplane piloted by a kamikaze pilot who has an inexplicable urge to land in the region under our child's soft palate; or it might be a train which tootles happily along a track before hurtling food into the dark tunnel that is Billy's oesophagus. These games are intended to make mealtimes more pleasurable and fun, though it's debatable for whom.

EXPERT VIEW

Distractions of this kind are unnecessary and complicate the eating process. Moreover, they could lead to psychological problems in later life. The child who needs this kind of encouragement is all very well, but the 40-year-old man who cannot consume a fish finger unless it's masquerading as a jumbo jet is just plain sad.

Limiting foods

If your child will only eat a few tried and tested foods, it's tempting to keep serving them up time and time again to the exclusion of all others. At least you know he or she is getting some nutrients, and the fact that these preferred foods are high in refined sugars, salt, saturated fats and the mystery ingredient which induces pimples is neither here nor there.

EXPERT VIEW

Presenting a very limited range of foods will only help to reinforce the child's dysfunctional diet. You must endeavour to serve up as many new foods as you can. Spend all day in a hot kitchen experimenting with a wide variety of nutritionally sound dishes and remember to smile when your child expresses his disapproval by feeding it all to the cat.

Distraction techniques

When a child is fearful or reluctant to try new foods, it can help to take his mind off the ordeal by having, say, a television, video recorder or radio playing in the background. While your diner is distracted, you may be fortunate enough to slip the odd crumb of a vol-au-vent, or soupçon of fromage frais between his unsuspecting lips.

Keep all distractions to a minimum as the entertainment may be more riveting than the food. In the worst-case scenario, the child may watch the whole of a cinematic epic while his food decomposes. Furthermore, if you have the audacity to cross his field of vision when attempting to feed him, you could unleash a major tantrum.

Can we do anything right?

There is a serious message to be gleaned from these examples. Don't dismiss any strategy or technique (with the exception of force feeding) if it shows the merest whisker of a chance of working with your child. And if all else fails, we could try to emulate some of the worst qualities that our offspring exhibit – by being equally stubborn and tenacious in our determination to get them to eat, we will win through in the end.

Everyone's an expert on the subject of diet and we've probably all heard variations on the following at some time or other. Invariably we're all too polite to say what we really think when people make thoughtless remarks about our children, but our alter egos might come up with some suitable responses.

Smart-alec friend:	He ate a whole sandwich today at my place. I can't see what the problem is.
Suggested response:	Make arrangements for a sleepover at their place in the near future. Catering for your darling at supper and breakfast should remove some of their cockiness.
Implied criticism:	You're clearly doing something wrong. The boy is perfectly all right with me.
Grandparents:	In my day, if we didn't eat what was on our plates for breakfast, it was served up again for dinner, and then again for supper. Parents today are too soft.
Suggested response:	How is Alfred's gastro-enteritis? It's a wonder any child of his generation got past puberty.

Implied criticism:	You're the author of your own misfortunes and a lousy mother to boot.

PTA leading light:	I don't know a single child who doesn't love my homemade cakes.
Suggested response:	You do now.
Implied criticism:	You're feeding him too many convenience foods. Good mothers consult cookbooks and do things the hard way.

Concerned neighbour:	I would be really worried if my child ate so little.
Suggested response:	If I were you, that would be the least of my worries.
Implied criticism:	You're clearly doing something wrong, but thankfully my brood are okay. I'm all right, Jack.

On a more serious note, we've all encountered someone who can destroy our fragile self-esteem with an ill-timed remark. One mother reported that she felt small and inadequate when a friend got her finicky son to eat a chocolate biscuit in her absence, then continued to crow about this feat whenever she had the opportunity. In all probability, this success would have been a flash in the pan and couldn't have been replicated in a fresh environment, but it was enough to instil a sense of failure in the mother concerned.

When parents have to cope with eating problems in addition to the difficulties of raising an autistic child, the last thing we need is a culture of blame. Although this attitude may be born of ignorance, it can still be incredibly hurtful. Sadly, it's often the members of our own families who fail to empathise with these difficulties. One mum in my sample confessed: 'I can't tell you how hurtful it was for me to be blamed, along with my husband, for my son's eating habits – the blame came from my parents, my sister, the school and…many others.' Whether real, or imagined, criticism of this nature is rarely constructive. Ideally, we should all be supporting the families and children affected by eating intolerances and looking for practical ways to overcome them.

4

Throw Out the Rule Book

When Jacky's a good boy,
He shall have cakes and custard;
But when he does nothing but cry,
He shall have nothing but mustard.
(*circa* 1815)

Even so-called normal children can give great cause for concern at meal-times. In *Toddler Taming*, Christopher Green noted:

> It is relatively easy to sit a child at the table and place food in front of him. Some clever parents can even get food into the reluctant child's mouth by using great feats of cunning, but no one has yet discovered the location of the switch that makes the toddler chew and then swallow the food. I am sure there is a Nobel Prize waiting for the person who discovers how to make toddlers eat. (Green 1984, p.42)

However, if your child is on the autistic spectrum you can multiply the difficulty of this exercise by several hundred. When parents have been unsuccessful in getting their child to try new foods, it's a logical progression to consult textbooks on the subject, or make an appointment to see an expert. Parents may have evolved the same strategies without any outside help – it's not rocket science – but sometimes a fresh input, using impressive charts and a stricter regulation of mealtimes, can succeed where we've failed.

However, in many cases, the distinctive nature of the autistic child is not taken into account when feeding strategies are recommended. The following techniques might well work with your average picky eater, but could fall short of the mark with a child on the autistic spectrum.

Involvement in meal preparation

The child is encouraged to choose foods in the supermarket, load them into the trolley, unpack them and become involved in the cooking process. This familiarity with foods is thought to lead to a greater inclination to try them, especially if the child has helped to create the end product, for example, by baking cakes.

> Our dietician thought that if Harry were involved in the baking of his own loaves, he might be more inclined to try bread products. We duly bought some bread mixes and encouraged him to get stuck in. Although he thoroughly enjoyed the process, the result was predictable. He had no intention of trying the end product as his underlying fear of bread had not been tackled. To his mind, eating bread would lead to sickness, and being involved in the creation of his own loaves did nothing to qualm these fears.

> Another mother told me that her son loved the idea of having his own trolley in the supermarket, choosing his own foods, and helping with meals, but she admitted, 'He doesn't eat what he chooses…and although he loves preparing food, he won't eat the finished product.'

Eat as a family

Mealtimes are generally seen as social occasions, and the standard advice is to eat as a family. Moreover, it is considered a bad idea to pander to individual food whims. Preferably, everyone at the table should be eating the same healthy, varied and nutritious range of foods.

When you have an extremely selective eater in the family, you may need to swap your existing oven for a double version to enable you to prepare two separate meals and still be able to eat en famille. It might also be advisable to place an order for a smaller table to place alongside the existing one, as your child may refuse to sit next to you if he/she can smell or see an item of food that offends. One family's health visitor thought that eating together would be a good idea: 'She suggested only offering our son what we were all having at mealtimes. We tried this a couple of times but he ended up eating nothing. We gave up late on the second day.' Possibly a bit more perseverance might have given better results, but this seemingly simple technique is anything but straightforward to implement in some families.

Peer pressure

It's widely assumed that picky eaters are influenced by watching other children eat. If they see their peers tucking into a wide selection of foods, they will want to join in, won't they?

The reverse may be the case with children on the autistic spectrum. If their senses are assailed by noisy diners eating a hotch-potch of disgusting items, the urge to join in might not be their number one coping strategy, whereas being sick might. When Harry attended his first kid's party, he saw it as an excellent opportunity to offload the items he didn't want onto his neighbour's plate.

Is my child an alien?

Every book I've consulted about faddy eaters, and believe me there have been quite a few, has stated the belief that no child would ever willingly starve themselves. However, some homilies have a pretty hollow ring when applied to the ASD child:

'After a few hours on fluids only, most children will have developed a very good appetite and will eat things that they wouldn't have dreamed of eating a few hours earlier' (Pearce 1991, p.37)

Many of these children do not appear to experience hunger as we know it, so removing food and waiting for them to beg for sustenance of any description may never happen. Indeed, they may call our bluff and doggedly refuse food for days on end. I was told that one little girl 'would rather starve than eat something she hasn't had before'. Another mum said, 'He doesn't appear to feel hunger to the same extent as others. He could go for long periods without food, and not be at all bothered. It is also very hard to get him to drink enough, since he doesn't seem to feel thirsty either.' Parents invariably worry if their children won't eat, but many children simply can't see what we're fussing about. When Harry was questioned by a health professional about the consequences of not eating, he coolly replied that he would 'get hungry'. He couldn't comprehend that there might also be a health risk involved. If your child goes on hunger strike, it is comforting to know that human beings can survive for a considerable period without food: 'It is possible for children to go without food for 10 hours for every year of life up to 5 years old without any problems' (Pearce 1991, p.36). However, it's essential to keep up fluid intake – we would all only survive a matter of hours without water.

Exploit their interests

If your son or daughter likes Thomas the Tank Engine, Pokemon characters or Postman Pat, experts may assume that your child will eat any foodstuffs in the shape of their favourite character. Undeniably this would be an attraction for most picky eaters, but will it pass muster with an ASD child?

We've purchased a wide variety of 'character meals' and snacks, but they haven't encouraged Harry to eat. Sometimes they have had the opposite effect. For example, as he has a tendency to take things literally, the prospect of eating a chocolate Santa from his Advent calendar made his extremely worried some years ago. 'I can't eat Santa,' he said logically, and I felt awful for even suggesting it.

Eat this and you'll grow up big and strong

Most children will relate to tales of Popeye thriving on a diet of spinach, and many will be enticed into eating their food if they think it will make them grow up big and strong like Daddy. But entreaties of this nature will only succeed if children want to change the way they look.

Some ASD children have a bit of a Peter Pan complex. If they don't like changes in general, why would they want their bodies to change as they grow? Harry has frequently told me that he likes being small and doesn't relish the idea of getting older or looking different. However, he isn't remotely interested in counting calories or whether foods are fattening, he simply eats what he likes. Another mum told me that her son 'doesn't want to grow and gets very upset that he will change size if he eats more'. This doesn't appear to be a calculated ploy to eat less; rather a statement that these children are quite happy with the way they are now, thank you.

Disguise it

Adding minute amounts of new foods to a child's preferred food will help to build up their tolerance of new tastes and textures, for example, vegetables like carrots and turnips could be disguised in a mashed potato mixture. Eventually, the child will eat larger and larger amounts of novel foods, and move on to eat a much wider diet.

We all have around 10,000 taste buds which allow us to distinguish between salty, sweet, sour and bitter tastes. Unfortunately, this fairly crude mechanism can be highly developed in some ASD children, particularly when it's teamed with ultra-sensitive olfactory nerves, the nose to you and me. In answer to the question 'Can I fool my highly sensitive child by hiding new foods in among the old?' I would suggest that the answer is an unqualified no. However, the success rate can go up dramatically with less discriminative subjects.

Educate your child

The general view is that the more your child knows about food and how it is processed by the body, the more inclined he or she will be to try it.

Moreover, a lecture or two on good and bad foods and how we need sustenance to survive should tip the balance in favour of adopting a healthy diet – in theory.

Whenever food science has been on the curriculum, Harry's concerns about what he's eating have increased. Things came to a head when he had to draw a diagram of the alimentary canal. He didn't want to know what happened to food once it had left his gullet, thank you very much, and this knowledge certainly didn't make him keen to try new foods – the reverse, in fact. Furthermore, when a child psychologist tried to impress on Harry the need to eat healthy foods to remain well, he concurred with her views and said he wanted to eat these items. Unfortunately, this said less about his desire to change his eating patterns, and rather more about his tendency to agree with whatever anyone suggested. When it came to the crunch, he had no intention of putting his words into practice.

Another mum explained that her son was fully clued up on the need to eat a healthy and varied diet, but was unable to translate the theory into practice: 'His tutor has done work with him on digestion and growth, so he knows the biological and logical commonsense, point of view. He's perfectly intelligent and able to understand it all, but still something stops him from eating. I don't think he knows what it is.'

Making choices

Some picky eaters are encouraged to choose the food they would like to eat. This tactic puts them in control of the eating process, and should encourage them to experiment with a wider range of foodstuffs.

If ASD children are asked to choose between a number of items for breakfast, the likelihood is that they would still be prevaricating at supper time. Questions such as 'Would you like porridge, or toast, dear?' will invariably be met with a blank stare, unless the child has an active dislike of what's on offer, in which case you will be rewarded with a response such as 'You must be joking'. Even the process of choosing a single item can be fraught with indecision. When Harry says he's hungry and I ask what he'd like to eat, he usually responds in the negative or throws the question back at me: 'What do you think I should have?' This game of verbal ping-pong can go on for ages:

'How about a banana?'

'No.'

'Cereal?'

'No.'

'Well, what would you like?'

'You decide.'

Once the ball is back in our court, we can cunningly opt for the lesser of two evils, for example, crisps rather than chocolate, so our children's indecisiveness may even be a blessing in disguise.

Simple bribery

This is undoubtedly a successful technique and has a high success rate with most children. However, there are always exceptions.

I've always considered Harry's problems to be fairly extreme. However, he has a good command of language, reads well and can be reasoned with on most topics. These factors have undoubtedly helped in our battle to increase his limited diet, but many children on the autistic spectrum are non-verbal and the simplest strategies can become incredibly complex.

> 'If she was verbal, I would offer her a treat such as some choco-late, a visit to the park, swimming, etc. as a means of encourag-ing her to eat. I'm sure this reward system could work well for some children, but probably not for children with severe forms of autism.'

Take your pick

Behavioural techniques to encourage our children to eat are broadly based on a series of positive or negative reinforcements. Although some

The Transport Museum in Covent Garden is one of Harry's
favourite places

parents have employed the latter to gain results (in its most extreme form, force feeding), it's widely believed that positive techniques are likely to be the most beneficial in encouraging our children to eat. When children show a heightened sensitivity to everything in their environment, it seems particularly cruel to employ bullyboy tactics to change their eating habits. There's always the danger that these techniques will serve to exacerbate the problem. Positive reinforcements may include verbal incentives such as praise for trying new foods, the offer of preferred foods once the child has tasted something new or a reward of some description.

Feeding clinics and some schools use *shaping* strategies to encourage children with eating intolerances to adopt a wider diet. This technique uses the softly, softly approach detailed in Chapters 13 and 14. Praise and a series of rewards are offered, for example, for acceptance of new foods on a plate; for letting the food touch the lips; then for allowing small amounts of food to be placed in the mouth; and finally for swallowing it. If these tactics are successful, the feeding prompts are gradually removed – a technique known as *fading*.

However, mild punitive techniques have also worked for some families. This may include the withholding of a treat until food has been eaten, for example, spending time on the computer or playing with a toy. Where there's a great deal of resistance to trying new foods, or where children express fear at mealtimes, *desensitisation* techniques may be employed. These take a variety of different forms, but the emphasis is on creating a stress-free eating environment with initially no pressure to ingest foods. Facial massage may be used to help a child with heightened sensitivity to touch. Gradually, foods are introduced, in conjunction with pleasant stimuli, to encourage a child to eat. Distraction techniques may also be employed to lessen the child's concerns about eating.

Some experts are very vocal in their dismissal of particular feeding strategies, for example, you should never offer rewards for eating, never give preferred foods for eating novel ones, never play games at mealtimes, etc. However, the ultimate litmus test is whether a strategy works. And if the answer is yes, then use it – without apology.

5

Survey Results

One, two, three, four,
Mary at the cottage door,
Five, six, seven, eight,
Eating cherries off a plate.
(*circa* 1815)

As the years went by and Harry's eating problems remained more or less the same, I realised that something had to be done, but was unsure what. We'd consulted our GP, a dietician, attended a paediatric feeding clinic, read everything we could on the subject, taken him to a cranial osteopath, and even for a series of healing sessions, but the great breakthrough we were hoping for had never materialised. Moreover, even though I knew other families were experiencing the same difficulties as us, I'd only met one comparable case through our local Asperger's group. The child concerned would only eat cold foods but was otherwise on a fairly healthy diet. If I could have persuaded Harry to drink fresh orange juice and milk, to eat raw vegetables and a selection of breads, cold meats, fruit and cereals, I think I would have been reasonably happy. So where were all these other faddy children and their parents?

*I don't mind sitting on a mushroom, but don't try sneaking any
on my plate.*

Questionnaire

In 1997, when Harry was seven-and-a-half, I drew up a basic questionnaire relating to eating disorders and placed notices in a number of publications inviting people to contact me if they could identify with the problem. The response was encouraging, but I had to renew my appeal on several occasions to build up a sample big enough to analyse and draw meaningful conclusions from. In total I mailed out around 120 questionnaires and received 89 back. Although statistically a small sample, it revealed some interesting findings.

Gender breakdown

The sample was made up predominately of male children, a total of 88.8 per cent, compared to just 11.2 per cent of females – a male to female ratio of almost 8:1. This figure wasn't really surprising as it reflects the higher incidence of ASD in the male population as a whole.

Daily menu

I asked parents to list the foods their children typically ate. Some children seemed to have a strong preference for carbohydrate-based foods, whereas others ate mainly protein, though in general meals were balanced, if rather limited. A number of favourites cropped up time and time again, with many children choosing turkey dinosaurs, fries, chicken nuggets, chipolata sausages, KitKats, Pringles crisps, smooth yogurts and fromage frais (no bits), pasta, dry cereal and tomato ketchup as their preferred foods. Rather than giving a meaningful insight into the autistic mind, I think this list probably gives an indication of the likes and dislikes of most youngsters in the general population.

However, very few children ate any vegetables at all. Again, this could reflect a broader trend, but research has shown that green vegetables can have a particularly bitter taste, so if children have highly sensitive taste buds they would naturally choose to avoid them. Perhaps this explains why Brussels sprouts were on most children's Ugh list. A number of children could tolerate carrots, tomatoes and sweetcorn, which don't have this disadvantage. Similarly, citrus fruits may taste unpleasant for the same reason. Perhaps it's not surprising that sweet fruits such as strawberries, melon and pears were among those generally liked.

As many ASD children are famed for liking bland products, it was a little surprising to discover that some had a preference for very strong tastes such as chilli and spicy curries. However, research conducted by scientists in France has shown that mothers who eat strong foods during pregnancy may influence their children's later preferences, as they become accustomed to these smells while in the womb (Schaal 2001). This evidence seems to suggest that our children's need for familiar tastes and smells is in evidence virtually from day one.

Medical diagnosis

I was keen to find out how many of the children were at the AS end of the continuum and how many had classic autism. However, the results should be interpreted with a degree of caution, as many children who were initially diagnosed as having autism were reclassified as having AS in later life. I discovered this anomaly when I conducted a brief follow-up with a control group taken from the original sample in 2001. However, taken at face value, the majority of children seemed to fall within the classic autism grouping:

classic autism	58.4%
AS	32.5%
others (including elements of ADHD, dyspraxia, etc.)	8.9%

This classification seems to be relevant when dealing with the psychology of a faddy eater. For example, peer pressure, and entreaties to eat to please another member of the family may be relevant to an AS child, who might actively want to make others happy. However, these tactics would cut no ice with a child with classic autism, who probably couldn't care less whether his actions pleased anyone or not.

When were feeding problems discovered?

Many parents were aware of problems from day one, but a cluster of eating difficulties seemed to occur around the 18-month mark. Some respondents couldn't pinpoint a specific time, and left this question blank:

0-1	37%
1-2	34.8%
2-3	17.4%
3-4	6.9%
4-5	0%
5-6	2.3%

I went on to enquire whether the problem had got worse over the years, improved or remained the same. The general trend suggests that the problem had worsened or remained more or less the same, but parents should take comfort from the fact that eating problems seem to peak in the one- to five-year age group. Evidence suggests things may improve in the long term:

Worse	47%
Better	18.8%
Same	34.1%

School-age children

Eating in a new environment can introduce a fresh set of problems. Invariably, the children who would accept school meals were the less faddy eaters. The ones who insisted on packed lunches were more likely to request the same items every day of the week and were particularly rigid in their attitude towards food:

School meals	33.8%
Packed lunches	64.5%
Other	1.6%

In answer to the question 'Did packed lunches vary from day to day, or remain the same?', 10 per cent of the sample said they did introduce some variety into these meals, whereas 90 per cent of the children ate the same foods on a regular basis.

Some children literally go on hunger strike if they have to eat away from home. One mum said, 'He rarely eats at school.' Another admitted, 'She leaves home at 8 am and returns at 4.15 pm. Most days she has eaten nothing in this period.' Some parents went to the trouble of preparing a packed lunch knowing that it would be returned in the same state at the end of the school day. One mum told me, 'She doesn't ever eat it. She eats nothing before 3 pm on weekdays and refuses any food at school.' One boy with AS duly took a packed lunch of butter and honey sandwiches to school each day and religiously brought them back. The accompanying chocolate biscuit, however, was generally eaten. His mother speculated that the chaos in schools at lunchtime could have been responsible for this, plus pressure from lunchtime staff to eat up, which invariably had the opposite effect. Another parent was more specific: 'He hates the smell of the school canteen and is put off by other children's eating habits and the type of sandwiches they eat. As a result, 90 per cent of the time he will only eat crisps at school, and doesn't touch his bottle of water, even though he requests it every day.' His sandwiches were invariably left to be eaten in the sanctuary of home. For other children, the lure of the playground was more important than refuelling on food: 'He doesn't eat well at school because he is too keen to get out and play,' said the mother of one young boy.

Conversely, some children eat well at school but not at home and the progression to trying school meals may be beneficial in some cases: 'The eating of school dinners seems to have coincided with less eating problems at home,' admitted one parent. At some schools, staff have evolved various eating programmes to help their pupils (see Chapter 14).

Outside help

Many parents have struggled on with their child's eating problems with no professional help. The reasons for this range from a general lack of confidence in specialists dealing with eating disorders to the belief that everything possible has already been tried at home and therefore nothing can be done. Of those who hadn't sought help, one mother simply commented: 'There's not much point is there?' Others are currently on waiting lists to see various specialists:

Received no help	32.1%
Consulted GP	10.7%
Dietician	35.7%
Eating disorder clinic	3.5%
Health visitor	5.9%
School	5.9%
Others	5.9%

Additional sources of help included a paediatrician, child psychologist, speech therapist, other parents and even a health food shop that ran tests for allergies. On the whole, parents were not over-impressed with the help they received. I asked them to evaluate how useful the specialist input had been.

Very useful	10.2%
Some help	32.6%
Made no difference	40.8%
Unhelpful	16.3%

One of the criticisms levelled at professionals was that the strategies they recommended were too general to help with the particular problems posed by children on the autistic spectrum. For instance, one mother said that the dietician she had consulted was able to reassure her that her son's diet was not lacking in essential vitamins and that his calorific intake was adequate, but was unable to offer practical advice to redress his limited interest in food. The boy also suffered from eczema and had an allergy to cow's milk and nuts. The dietician tended to focus on these areas but 'did not take into account the influence of his autism on why he wasn't eating, concentrating more on what his allergies would allow him to eat'. Yet another respondent simply wrote the word 'useless' against the dietician category.

Another complaint was that GPs didn't always seem to take the problem seriously, especially if the child seemed to be developing normally in other ways. One parent was advised by a speech therapist that desensitisation techniques might help her son who reacted to some foods by gagging and being sick. However, her GP wouldn't make the necessary referral as he couldn't accept there was anything wrong.

Furthermore, if the problem is recognised it tends to be written off far too lightly for some parents' tastes:

> My GP told me not to worry about…diet, and that he was most probably getting enough nutrients. When I mentioned that my son ate dirt, he also told me not to worry about it as it was just part of his condition…but I obviously *do* worry about these things.'

One mother said, 'In the past we've seen nutritionists, doctors, and hospital specialists, but nobody helped.' Another complained that her doctor had threatened to put her three-year-old son in hospital because he was underweight – this practice has largely died out now, except in the most extreme cases.

Dietary supplements

In this section I enquired whether children were taking any supplements to make up for deficiencies in their diets:

Vitamin supplements	54.6%
Calcium	12.7%
Neither	39.5%

Although children on a restricted diet may need dietary supplements, it's no simple matter to get them to take them, so I wasn't surprised to find that almost 40 per cent of the sample took no extra pills or potions to improve their diet. Many of the supplements commonly prescribed for children have unacceptably strong tastes and trying to persuade a child who hates 'bits' and lumps that they should swallow a tablet for their own good merits a chapter on its own: I suspect that the children who could be persuaded to take supplements had discovered one of the few flavourless and therefore relatively innocuous versions on the market, more of which later.

Food qualities

This section provided some interesting insights into what our children really think about the food we present them with. If you have heightened senses, the whole eating process becomes incredibly complicated. Many children simply couldn't contemplate tasting something if it smelt or looked unappetising, or had the wrong texture. In one case, food even had to be described in the correct order or it would be rejected at the dinner table. For example, this particular boy quite liked fishfingers, chips and beans, but if his mother said that beans, chips and fishfingers were on the menu, the food would be rejected because, according to his logic, it wasn't fishfingers, chips and beans. I asked parents to rate their children's dietary preferences in order of importance (1–6), based on the following criteria and the results were as follows:

Appearance	1
Texture	2
Taste	3
Smell	4
Familiar packaging	5
Gimmicks, e.g. free toys with cereal	6

The results placed taste and texture almost neck and neck and smell and familiar packaging were just a few points apart. However, appearance retained a firm lead, which contradicts some of the current literature on ASD which rates texture as being the most important factor overall.

Appearance

The look of food has played a large part in my son's acceptance or rejection of meals. Even favourites such as nuggets and chips will be cast aside if they've been slightly overcooked, have too many 'bits' or are a strange colour. One of the main stumbling blocks to getting our children to try something new is that they can show great intolerance to anything unfamiliar. In some cases, a little ritual has to be performed before food can be eaten. One mother told me:

> If my son eats crisps, you have to open the packet a particular way, and it must be a blue packet or he won't eat them. KitKats must be broken a certain way, and he has to have the wrappers laid out flat next to him to read as he eats. Tomato sauce must be in a bowl beside food, not on it…plates have to be turned around to face a certain way, as do bottles and cups and cutlery.

Here are some of the comments other parents have made about how food should look:

> She doesn't ask for food by name but will request a particular shape, colour, or type of packaging, for example, 'blue crisps' when she wants the salt and vinegar variety. Rather than asking for a fishfinger, she'll say she 'wants rectangle'.

> Appearance is very important. He won't even try something that doesn't look right.

> Food always has to look the same. If his toast is too brown it will be refused.

> He will only eat food if it's cut into certain shapes – toast must be in squares or triangles. Spaghetti will only be eaten if it's short and in tomato sauce.

Since starting school, he has found black 'bits' in most foods and refuses to eat them. Now he looks for green 'bits' as well. He can see them even if they are microscopic and refuses to have different foods on the same plate because they then become 'contaminated'.

My son will only eat and drink certain foods from a particular plate or cup. He has one cup for milk, another for orange juice, etc.

[He] will simply not entertain anything that *looks* different on his plate. It has taken years for him to try a different make of cocktail sausage, even though they all look identical to me.

There is a genuine fear of food. It's not that he doesn't want to try it, sometimes his whole body is arching away because of something I've put in front of him.

For several years my son would eat from three separate plates to make sure no items touched each other.

Chips can't be eaten if they're a funny shape or look a bit odd. He likes them to be almost symmetrical. They have to be the same size and shape to please him.

Sausages must be sliced and not served whole, otherwise they won't be eaten.

He would only eat certain Alphabites (potato shapes) – the ones which didn't have any enclosed spaces. For example, he would eat T, H and S, but not O, A and B.

Texture

A universal hatred of 'bits' and lumps seem to be the norm for the kids in my sample. In this case, two categories overlap – the diners can't bear to look at these imperfections and they certainly don't want to put them in their mouths. Bland, smooth textures are invariably favoured over lumpy, inconsistent ones. However, some children actively seek out crunchy foods and many show a preference for dry foods over wet ones:

She tends to like crunchy foods, e.g. toast. It needs to be almost incinerated, then buttered once it's cool, or she will say 'it's soggy' and spit it out.

He will not eat eggs in *any* way, shape or form because he doesn't like the texture.

He hates sloppiness, i.e. gravy, milky things and soups. He won't have eggy foods unless they are well mixed and almost burnt.

My son has a dislike of soft, savoury foods like fresh meat and vegetables. I think it is a texture dislike because he likes the taste of chicken in chicken nuggets, but he won't eat fresh chicken. He likes crunchy foods and will eat chips or potato waffles, but he won't eat mashed or boiled potatoes.

She won't eat anything with a texture that she finds strange. She will physically gag if you put eggs or bananas anywhere near her, and won't eat yogurt or ice cream if it has any trace of a lump in it.

He hates slimy, lumpy and varied textures. He likes textures to be uniform.

My son doesn't bite or chew food. He swallows whatever he is given whole, so it must be a smooth texture.

He will always *feel* his food, especially if it's unfamiliar, before he'll put it to his mouth. If he doesn't like the feel of it, he won't even try it.

Very occasionally he will take, literally, a teaspoonful of homemade lentil soup. It must be liquidised, then sieved. Despite this, he finds 'bits' in it and says the texture is not smooth enough for him.

I recently slipped a piece of chicken nugget into his mouth, in between mouthfuls of chips. When he found it required more chewing than the chips, he had a real panic attack.

He knows the difference between different brands of wholemeal bread by their texture.

He hates anything slimy, for example, pasta or fruit in yogurt, and prefers crunchy textures like cereals and crisps.

If he eats anything that he believes to be smooth and discovers bits in it, e.g. yogurt, he will vomit.

My son hates sloppy foods. He won't eat his cereal if it is left in milk too long as it becomes soggy.

The texture of food is very important. He will not eat anything soft or mushy, such as mashed potatoes.

Taste

For our children to be willing to taste food, it must already have passed a number of important hurdles. Even if food looks acceptable, seems to smell okay and has a uniform texture, it may still take an enormous leap of faith actually to place that food in your mouth, and once there, the chances of it being swallowed may be pretty remote:

Everything that [he] eats is pecked at, like a bird. When he eats a banana, we very gently wipe a little across a bottom front tooth so that just a tiny bit sticks. This 'piece' is then eaten. It will take him around 30 minutes to eat about an inch, the rest is then discarded.

Will not eat food if the recipe has changed, even slightly, to alter the taste.

He loves the taste of taramosalata and hummus and will dip all his food in the latter.

Although he generally likes bland foods, he sometimes surprises me by requesting quite spicy things. At our local farmer's market, he always makes a beeline for the curry paste stall and tries all the different flavours, including the very hot ones.

He likes some quite strong tastes and will only eat mature cheese.

He is unwilling to even taste anything different. If I put a sample of something that we are eating on his plate, he either takes it off or throws it away.

Very acute sense of taste, for example, we cannot 'hide' medicines in his drinks or food.

My son likes very strong garlic and onion flavours, particularly Loyd Grossman sauces, and although I have tried to replicate the flavour, he knows the difference.

He is hypersensitive to taste. If you add even half a teaspoon of another foodstuff to his usual food, he will refuse it.

Loves sweet things, even ginger or cinnamon spices are acceptable if there is enough sugar on the food. Also, he likes chilli hot things and salty and fatty things.

He is very specific about certain types of taste. Like his father and I, he cannot bear any type of spicy food, but will eat things with herbs, like spaghetti bolognese.

As she becomes older, she is more willing to try a small taste of something which wouldn't previously have made it into her mouth.

Smell

We all react to the smell of food to some degree. The smell of freshly baked bread and coffee appeals to most of us and if a meal 'smells good' it's a pretty good indication that it will taste good too. However, to some children on the autistic spectrum, the association between smell and taste seems to be a bit more complicated. For instance, they may appreciate the smell of something, but still have no intention of trying it. Moreover, if their sense of smell is particularly acute, they're more likely to dwell on the negative aspects of food rather than the positive:

He will not eat with us if there is food with a strong smell in the room, e.g. fish, curry, pot noodles. He won't feed the cat because of the smell of cat food.

The smell of food is his main problem. He seems to have a really sensitive nose and can smell onion, cucumber, fruit, etc. if he is two rooms away. As a small child, he would vomit if anybody was eating anything he disliked nearby.

Will say things smell horrible and refuse to eat them, when they smell quite normal to me.

He refers to most foods and drinks as being 'stinking'.

My son has a bad reaction to the smell or sight of cut fruit. It makes him gag and he will run away if he sees it.

Smell is *so* important. If I add a different ingredient to food, e.g. mixed herbs to chicken dishes, it will not be eaten.

If he doesn't like the smell, then he isn't going to eat it. He dislikes strong or 'horrid' things and smells everything before it goes into his mouth.

He is revolted by the smell of cooked fish and vegetables.

Smells most things before he eats them. He always has to have pure sunflower spread and can immediately tell by the smell if it's the wrong sort.

Will often smell foods before he'll try them. He is very sensitive to the smell of cooking and if he doesn't like the food is quite disturbed by it.

Familiar packaging

Parents of food phobic kids have an unabashed hatred for trendy marketing men who spend all their working lives coming up with clever new ideas for familiar products. Fresh logos, revamped packages and, worst of all, 'new, improved' recipes are the bane of our lives. It takes a lot of time and effort to acclimatise our children to various products and

just when we've struck gold, some smart marketing man comes along
and changes the look of them:

> He used to like a particular pack of crisps but they've intro-
> duced a special range with a different picture on the front and
> he won't eat them now.

> My son will only eat certain brands of food, often those he has
> seen advertised on TV. If there is any change to the packaging,
> even something as small as a price alteration, he will not eat it
> again.

> Will not eat products if the appearance is changed in any way.
> When they changed the wrapper on his favourite chocolate
> bars he wouldn't eat them any more.

> They changed the packaging on chocolate fingers and, even
> though we explained that the product would taste exactly the
> same, he would never try them again.

> Familiarity is what he likes and requires in all his food.

> Food has to look the same every time. If there is a change in
> packaging, or an improved recipe, we have to reintroduce the
> food or hide the packet.

> When shopping, he looks out for packets he knows. If we select
> any others, he turns away. My son doesn't speak, so he turns to
> look at or points to the products he wants.

> He feels reassured by familiar logos and is more likely to eat a
> food if he associates a picture with it.

> Packaging in itself isn't as important as particular brands,
> although when packaging is changed she does take some con-
> vincing that it is the same product.

Gimmicks

In the grand scheme of things, gimmicks were considered to be relatively unimportant. However, many children have badgered their

parents to buy them a foodstuff with a coveted giveaway at some stage, and the parents have relented in the hope that their son or daughter would actually eat the cereal/ice lollies/crisps, or whatever. More often than not, the kids will gleefully accept the gift, then refuse point-blank to have anything to do with the edibles:

> My son will select foods that look attractive or come with a free toy, but he won't actually try them.

> Gimmicks simply don't apply. He has resolutely stuck to the same foods since he was tiny and will not try anything new.

> He will eat almost any cereal to get a free toy. However, sometimes I'll buy a particular product and he doesn't like the taste, so it's wasted.

> On the whole, I try to avoid buying these, but I think he could be encouraged to eat a food if it came with a toy – that is, if he wasn't so distracted by the toy that he ignored the food!

> He is quite obsessed with buying food with gimmicks, but this would not persuade him to eat the contents.

> When he was younger, I would always have to buy the cereal that had a free toy, rather than his usual brand. Then there was a promotion with World Cup coins and I had to buy lots of items that featured them – but someone else in the household had to eat the food.

When parents have to consider all the variables above, it's a wonder that our children ever eat anything. The extreme sensitivity exhibited by many selective eaters presents a whole new set of problems:

- Is it wise to force our ideas of a balanced diet onto these children when some foods clearly repulse them?

- Are we doing more harm than good when we insist that they try a morsel of a food we think they should be eating?

- Might we put them off food for life by demanding that they try new things?

- Is our insistence that they should broaden their diets for
  their convenience or ours?

There are no clear answers to these questions, but the most compelling arguments suggest that we shouldn't be heavy handed in our approach to this problem and should never force the issue of eating if it causes undue distress to our children. These are the guidelines that come across in the strategies employed in the following chapters.

6

Hints and Tips

I'll have none of your nasty beef,
Nor I'll have none of your barley;
But I'll have some of your very best flour
To make a white cake for my Charley.
(*circa* 1748)

There can be few things more irritating than having someone say 'Have you tried this?' when your child won't eat. The implication is that you are content to sit back and do nothing while your son or daughter wastes away before your eyes. In fact, parents of children with eating intolerances have had to evolve a wide variety of strategies to cope with the problem and are probably far more qualified to offer advice in this area than many professionals.

Dr Lorna Wing commented in the Foreword to *The World of the Autistic Child* (Siegal 1996): 'Parents of children with autistic spectrum disorders…do not, in general, have a high opinion of professionals.' To some extent I share these misgivings, but I do have great faith in parents who have to deal with this distressing problem on a daily basis. Coping with a child with eating intolerances is incredibly difficult and can be demoralising. One parent admitted to me, 'We have given up trying to introduce new foods.' In general, the mood of the parents taking part in my survey has been very upbeat and hopeful.

In one section of my questionnaire I asked parents to list the foods their child ate. The responses were wide ranging – in one instance 60 items of food were catalogued and 11 types of beverage. Clearly the parents thought their child had a problem, but for the purposes of this small sample I thought it best to concentrate on the children who had a relatively small intake of foods. At the other end of the spectrum were several children who had a total food intake of no more than three or four items. Invariably, the parents of these children left the 'tips' part of the survey blank. One parent wrote: 'At the moment [he] has a complete aversion to all food, he doesn't even want food near him.' Clearly, some of these parents were at the end of their tether, having tried all sorts of remedies with little or no success. As one mum put it:

> We have tried bribery, mixing foods, threats, rewards, eating in different places, and making lists of foods. We have tried having other children around at mealtimes and try to get…to join in, but she doesn't. She stopped eating at school when they tried to insist she ate more. Nothing works. In fact the more we try to get her to eat, the less she will do it.

Faced with this kind of opposition, it's no wonder that parents feel less than enthusiastic when someone suggests yet another strategy. However, I firmly believe that things can change for the better, even in the most severe cases. Here are some tips that have worked for other families. Give them a try, they may work with your child.

CASE 1

DIAGNOSIS: AS

This young boy has a general lack of interest in food, which has proved very difficult to deal with, despite numerous interventions by his family. He has always been small for his age and, like my son, had the distinction of being the oldest boy in his class at school but also the smallest. His intake of foods can be counted on one hand and he tends to have a sweet tooth.

TIPS

- Watching cartoons in the morning is a treat, so he is allowed to eat Cocopops while they're on. If I'm not happy with what he's eaten, the TV goes off for one minute. I use a timer which bleeps when the minute is up so he knows exactly how long it is. If things don't improve, I might say, 'If I have to turn the TV off the next time, it will be for two minutes', etc. This technique has been quite successful.

- I present him with a tray with a savoury item (no junk foods), and a sweet item. The rule is: sweet things *last*. This can encourage him to eat the less pleasant item *first*.

- Goal cards – as used in Applied Behaviour Analysis (ABA), where skills are learnt by being broken down into small, manageable steps. The cards are blank and the size of a business card. They can be used for a variety of behavioural targets, including eating. For example, on one side you write a series of goals, e.g. eat breakfast, get dressed, clean teeth – 8.30 am latest. On the reverse side are two alternative sets of consequences for compliance and non-compliance; the former is illustrated by a smiley face, the latter by a sad face. The reward or punishment is then written next to the appropriate face, e.g. ten tokens (plastic money) for good behaviour which can be used to 'buy' treats like books, chocolate or games kept in a special 'reward' cupboard. Bad behaviour can result in a 'fine,' collected in tokens, or the withholding of a treat.

- A small palmtop computer can be used in the same way as the goal cards. Behavioural goals are set and monitored, then rewards or punishments meted out as appropriate.

- Eating is sometimes seen as a distraction which stops him vocalising his thoughts and ideas, so we set up a dictaphone to record any ideas he had at mealtimes.

CASE 2

DIAGNOSIS: AS

This teenage boy has a preference for carbohydrates and convenience foods: crisps, cornflakes, muesli bars and biscuits make up a significant part of his diet.

TIPS

- Will sometimes eat more successfully when distracted, i.e. when watching television or talking to someone.

- Eats normally when in the company of guests because he is terrified of being considered to be strange or different.

CASE 3

DIAGNOSIS: AS/ADD

On paper, this boy seems to eat a fairly wide diet, including bread, cereals, pasta, pizza, nuggets and chips. The diet is largely carbohydrate based, though he gets protein from milk, cheese and some meat products.

TIPS

- Bribery tied in with his interests, e.g. if you eat your dinner for a whole week you can have a new game for your Game Boy.

- Offer meal options with the proviso that he must eat one vegetable out of the following, e.g. carrots, broccoli, green beans. He sometimes responds to the choice element of this.

- Every four days he may be allowed one 'cheat' dinner – i.e. something he really likes/wants. For the first three days he has to eat our choice of food for him; then on the fourth day he can choose, for example, cornflakes for dinner. He usually responds quite well to this.

CASE 4

DIAGNOSIS: AS

This young boy follows a fairly rigid and restricted diet with a preference for dry, crunchy foods. He will only tolerate juice in a carton with a straw.

TIP

- To get around his dislike of 'wet' food, e.g. cereal with milk added, I give him a portion of Weetabix with milk, then sprinkle Cocopops on top to give a crunchy element to the food.

CASE 5

DIAGNOSIS: AS/IBS

This older boy has a diet which seems to have improved over the years – aged two, he would only eat six foods and they all had to be white. Now he will accept most types of meat, potatoes, rice, pasta, bread, cereals and a range of desserts. However, he won't eat any fish products and the only vegetables he likes are potatoes.

TIPS

- Establishing a clear routine can help and meals and snacks are always at regular times.

- It can be difficult to eat together as a family but I adapt meals accordingly so he always has things he likes. For example, if spaghetti bolognese is on the menu, he simply has spaghetti and grated cheese. If I cook hotpot or shepherd's pie, I make sure one end has no vegetables so my son will eat it too.

CASE 6

DIAGNOSIS: AUTISTIC

This young boy exists mainly on a diet of porridge with mashed banana, peanut butter sandwiches, Marmite sandwiches, Marmite and a limited variety of snacks.

TIPS

- We try not too put too much pressure on him and have realistic expectations about what he will and won't eat. Follow the Lovaas programme[1] for general behavioural control – this promotes the need to ignore bad behaviour and reward good.

CASE 7

DIAGNOSIS: AUTISM WITH SEVERE RECEPTIVE LANGUAGE DELAY

A fan of strong flavours, such as garlic and onion, this young boy eats a reasonably varied diet but consumes an above average amount of milk – around three to four litres a day. He goes through phases of eating a lot on some occasions, his mum describes it as 'stoking up', then eats relatively little for several days.

TIPS

- If the main meal is rejected, we tempt him into eating by introducing foods which are currently in favour, e.g. sausage rolls or crisps. He doesn't mind what order he eats in and will frequently go from savoury to sweet foods in alternate mouthfuls.

- Foods like spaghetti bolognese have to be mashed up to appeal to him. If he still won't try it, we add something he

---

1   Ivor Lovaas is a Norwegian psychologist who evolved a programme to help autistic children on a one-to-one basis. The programme focuses on early intervention and reward strategies to modify behaviour. Treatments use the principles of Applied Behaviour Analysis (ABA).

really likes, e.g. bread sticks, and he will eat the mixture like a dip.

- Foods such as bread, cake and banana, are more acceptable if they are cut into bite-sized pieces. Sometimes he will eat pieces of banana off a fork.

- He drinks a great deal which can fill him up very quickly and take away his appetite. To get around this problem, we tend to give him tiny amounts of juice at mealtimes. These have to be topped up frequently between mouthfuls of food.

CASE 8

DIAGNOSIS: AUTISM

One of the most severe cases, this boy followed a very restricted diet when I first sent the family a questionnaire in 1999, though he was accepting a variety of fruits in liquidised form. In the meantime, the diet has deteriorated even further and he has had three hospital admissions in the space of five months. Now his food intake consists solely of yogurt and milk, though he will take multivitamin and mineral supplements.

TIP

- Music has been all-important in helping our son to eat. In the early days, we put on a tape of Postman Pat stories. Once he started to eat, it was changed to a nursery rhyme tape. If he refused to eat, we went back to the original tape. Later, Postman Pat became redundant and we were able to play nursery rhymes only. Now we don't play tapes, but if he refuses food we just sing the songs.

CASE 9

DIAGNOSIS: ASD

This boy will eat a few staple foods such as pasta, chips and cereal and has a liking for savoury snacks and biscuits.

TIP

- We try to give a particular food up to two or three times a week in the hope that he will eventually come to accept it. If we were to offer a new food just once a week, he would never accept it. Familiarity with foods, as with everything else in his world, makes our son feel safe.

CASE 10

DIAGNOSIS: AUTISM, EPILEPSY, LEARNING DIFFICULTIES

This boy was born three months prematurely and has had eating problems from birth. He eats a variety of cereals and will try school dinners and puddings, toast, beans, pasta, chips, fishfingers and beef-burgers, though his mother added the comment 'sometimes' to many of the items on his list of preferences.

TIP

- A homeopathic remedy called Ignatia has had limited success, which is simply added to his milk.

CASE 11

DIAGNOSIS: AUTISTIC TENDENCIES (POSSIBLY AS), PERVASIVE DEVELOPMENTAL DISORDER (PDD)

This little girl is very resistant to new foods. She will eat cold chicken if it's served at grandma's house, but not at home. All her likes revolve around cold foods. She has never eaten a hot meal.

TIPS

- Make up stories as she's eating, usually about favourite TV characters

- She has an interest in numbers so we use this imagery to encourage eating, i.e. eat three more X and you can have Y.

- Similarly, time can be an incentive (she could tell 24 hour time at the age of 2), so instructions to eat a particular item and you can have more at, say, 3.30 pm can be effective.

Generally these strategies work only with familiar foods; introducing new ones is much more difficult.

CASE 12

DIAGNOSIS: ASD

To compound his dietary problems, this young boy will only eat food off the floor. He has a preference for cold foods and although he likes chips, he will leave them to get cold before he can eat them.

TIP

- Likes Twiglets, so a friend suggested trying Marmite sandwiches as the yeast taste is similar. This was a limited success; he ate two over a period of two weeks.

CASE 13

DIAGNOSIS: ASD, CROHN'S DISEASE

TIPS

- Loves sweet things, so the promise of these can work as an incentive to try other foods.

- Putting extra food on my plate can help. He will sometimes eat from this rather than his own.

CASE 14

DIAGNOSIS: AS, DYSPRAXIA

This girl has a preference for protein-based foods and will eat a wide range of meat products. Problems seemed to be in evidence right from the start. She refused solids up to the age of eight months. She currently likes fish, but only from a particular shop and with the batter removed.

TIPS

- Vegetables are eaten in very small amounts only. The best results are gained by offering a small portion. Then we

negotiate about how much of the food will be eaten –
usually around two-thirds. If she were expected to eat it all,
she would end up eating very little.

CASE 15

DIAGNOSIS: COMMUNICATION DISORDER

WITH AUTISTIC TENDENCIES

This boy is of primary school age but still has a liking for some baby
foods. His diet includes chips, pasta, white bread and a variety of snack
foods. It was mentioned that his dad had a very selective diet that lasted
from childhood until the teen years.

TIP

- The school laminates pictures of the foods he eats and
  mounts them in a photograph album with Velcro fasteners.
  When he wants something, he has to present the picture of
  the item in exchange for the real thing. The aim is to
  increase communication and slowly introduce pictures of
  food we would like him to eat.

CASE 16

DIAGNOSIS: AUTISTIC

This boy follows one of the most limited diets of all those surveyed. He
eats between four to six small pots of fromage frais per meal. If distracted, he will eat a small amount of Ready Brek cereal. He doesn't bite
or chew, but swallows foods whole.

TIP

- Distraction techniques, e.g. feeding him while a favourite TV
  show is on.

CASE 17

DIAGNOSIS: AS

A vegetarian, in common with the rest of his family, he is served the same foods as everyone else and is neither praised for finishing foods, nor chastised for leaving them. On schooldays he will eat large amounts of cereal. His mother speculates this may be (a) because it delays the start of the school day; and (b) it fills him up so he needn't worry about having to eat in a different environment – he invariably eats very little at school.

TIPS

- We stress that it's his choice what he eats, so he's never under pressure at mealtimes.

- If food is presented in 'finger' form it's more likely to be eaten. He says he dislikes cheese but if it's added to savoury scones cut into fingers he will eat it.

- Homemade biscuits are shaped into fingers and vegetarian sausages and burgers are also presented in this way.

- Homemade cheesecake is acceptable if it's given a new name so he's not aware he's eating cheese. My version, containing ricotta cheese, is called Moussecake.

- Hates lumpy food so I make homemade soup with lots of veg and purée it. Whatever sort I make, it's always given the same name GFU, (Good for You) soup, so there's a psychological impetus to eat it.

- He's invariably happiest eating when he has a book at his side, so we allow this.

- If he chooses to eat the pudding first, that's fine. More often than not he'll return to the main meal, then back to the dessert.

CASE 18

DIAGNOSIS: AS

This boy had feeding problems from birth and didn't take well to being breast fed, though his mother persevered for several months. In general, dietary problems have improved with age as his communication skills have developed. He now eats a fairly wide range of foods, including hot and spicy things like chilli. Paradoxically, he will also eat frozen peas, both cold and cooked.

TIPS

- My child loves language, rhymes and ditties, so I make up short stories or songs about the food I want him to eat. For example, if broccoli is on the menu, I'll say, 'Look, here is the tiny tree in the tiny forest where the tiny birds are roosting; eat it up so the birds will be safe.' I also modify Bob Dylan lyrics to encourage him to eat green beans, 'Give me a bean – I'm a hungry man. A shotgun fired and away I ran'. Maybe this works because of the repetitive element of rhyme – it feels safe and predictable, and perhaps these qualities become associated with the food.

- I make animal shapes of different food – gratifying his obsessional interest in animals.

- Portions are kept relatively small, so he doesn't get visually distracted and manages to clear his plate so feels he has successfully completed his task/activity.

- I offer tangible rewards for eating things he doesn't like – i.e. the reward biscuit, ice-cream, or whatever must be right in front of him to keep the thing meaningful. It's no good simply saying 'you can have an ice cream when you've eaten that'. He has to see it.

- A textbook eating rule is that families should eat together, but we try to be flexible on this. He may be adverse to sitting down to meals with the family and run off after 'picking' at food. I accept this and it takes the pressure off him. If he likes the food enough he may come back after we've finished our food and eat alone. Eating is not a time to be sociable for our son, it's simply what he does to re-fuel.

- In common with many autistic children, my son is unhappy about using cutlery. He uses his fingers and I don't make a fuss about this. Eating in this way seems to reassure him that the temperature and texture of the food are satisfactory before he puts it in his mouth.

- Whenever I feel he hasn't been eating enough, or is eating too much of the same things, I draw up a list of the things he is eating, things he used to eat and two new things I'd like him to eat. Even if I don't succeed in getting him to eat the new things, the simple act of writing things down is beneficial. Usually I feel surprised by how much he does eat – it helps me to get things in perspective.

CASE 19

DIAGNOSIS: AUTISM

This boy follows a reasonably varied diet, incorporating items from all the main food groups. He used to eat from a plate on the floor.

TIPS

- If he tries a new food, we praise him for his efforts. In order to get him to try the same food again, we would need to produce it again either on the same day, or the next. This immediacy seems to be crucial. If we left it a week or more, he would be unlikely to co-operate and try it again.

- Throughout the day we also remind him of how good he was to try something new, which makes him happy. We may ask him to help carry an object, e.g. bucket of Lego, and tease him by saying, 'I bet you can't carry that.' Once he responded with 'I can, I ate a new food today, and now I've got big muscles.' We reinforced this idea with, 'Yes, you're getting big and strong like Dad because you ate a new food.' We then gave him a treat.

- Since colour is also very important, we show him the container that, say, pot noodles come in, so he can approve it. For example, the chicken and mushroom flavour comes in a green tub. Once he has seen this he is more prepared to eat the contents.

CASE 20

DIAGNOSIS: ASD

This boy had dietary problems right from the start. He suffered from reflux and had to have Gaviscon mixed with his feed for several months. He hates spicy food but will tolerate meals with herbs in.

TIPS

- Healthy foods are disguised as things he likes, for example, I serve up vegetable grills containing rice, vegetables and herbs and call them burgers to appeal to him. I also make my own spaghetti bolognese, macaroni cheese and carbonara pasta so I can add lots of things that are good for him, e.g. garlic, without him knowing.

- I also adapt things to tie in with his interests, for instance, pink custard (made with a milkshake mix) becomes Tubby Custard as he's a Teletubby fan. Similarly, muffins are Tubby Toast. As he loves farm animals, malted milk biscuits are a winner; he thinks of them as 'special cow biscuits'.

CASE 21

DIAGNOSIS: SPECIFIC SPEECH AND LANGUAGE DISORDER

ATYPICAL AUTISM

This girl will not eat any fruit or salad but her diet has improved a little over the years. Favourite items include chicken, pork, sausages, potatoes, baked beans, cheese, Marmite and carrots.

TIP

- I make a bargain with her that she must try new foods but initially she only has to sniff them and put her tongue on them. Then she has to try a tiny amount. She will do this but insists on having a glass of water to wash down the food if she doesn't like it.

CASE 22

DIAGNOSIS: SEVERE SPEECH, LANGUAGE AND COMMUNICATION PROBLEMS, AUTISM AND TOURETTE'S SYNDROME

This boy's problems with food were discovered when he was around four months old and have changed little over the years. However, he eats quite a wide range of fruits and will try toast, pizza and pasta, several types of meat and baked beans. He has a preference for cold foods and likes to douse hot food in tomato ketchup.

TIPS

- Peer pressure works with my son. If I get him to eat with other children, his food intake increases.
- We also discuss good and bad foods. We draw two circles and my son puts good foods in one, e.g. pasta, bread, milk, apples and bad foods in the other, e.g. chocolate, cake, biscuits, fizzy pop. This encourages him to try the former.

CASE 23

DIAGNOSIS: AUTISTIC WITH SPEECH AND LANGUAGE PROBLEMS

This boy's diet is predominately carbohydrate based, including things such as pasties, biscuits, crisps and chocolate cake. His mother comments that apparently he eats well at school.

TIP

- If he doesn't want his dinner I give it to the dog, and he's not allowed anything until the next meal time.

CASE 24

DIAGNOSIS: UNDIAGNOSED

This girl has a reasonably balanced diet but tends to favour protein. She eats a wide range of meats and cheeses. Her main difficulty seems to be concentrating at mealtimes. She's easily distracted and may need to be reminded to eat.

TIPS

- The promise of doing an activity that motivates her after a meal can help her to eat.

- Playing a game we call 'acting out the story being told by Dad', with her as the central character. Sometimes this may involve the character trying a new food, but it tends to be more successful in encouraging her to go to bed; e.g. 'Once upon a time there was a little girl called . . . and she was so tired that when it was bedtime she went straight away.'

CASE 25

DIAGNOSIS: AS

This boy's eating problems were discovered when he was around seven months old. There has been a gradual improvement in his diet over the years, but he still prefers a fairly bland diet and tends to avoid spicy foods.

TIPS

- His preference for sweet things is an incentive for him to finish the main meal.

- Finishing quickly makes him feel good; he thinks he's ahead of the competition.

- Starting school dinners seems to have helped him to experiment more at home.

- To minimise stress, we try to introduce new things during a relaxed period, e.g. holidays. There is no tension associated with the rest of the day and no time limitations on finishing food. An extra incentive is usually provided to finish new foods.

- We encourage him to eat a variety of foods by stipulating that breakfast should not be the same day after day and he must eat a variety of things at dinnertime to help him grow. If he leaves a familiar food, he doesn't get a pudding. Finally, he must at least try everything.

CASE 26

DIAGNOSIS: AUTISTIC

This boy follows a diet that is almost exclusively carbohydrate based; crackers, biscuits, breadsticks, cereal bars and cake feature strongly in his meals. He drinks a lot and will try lemonade, cola, orange squash, fresh juice and milk. He has a general dislike of hot foods.

TIP

- He has been tempted to try some food which his younger brother is eating, though this is a rarity. Eating together as a family is generally helpful.

CASE 27

DIAGNOSIS: AS

This boy is quite happy to eat the same foods for breakfast, dinner and tea. He has a liking for KFC and tries to replicate the recipe and presentation of his favourite meal at home. He seemed to eat most things as a toddler, so in some ways his diet has worsened with time.

TIP

- Try to restrict the number of snacks he eats. If I can stop him snacking before dinner, he will usually eat the whole meal – a cause for celebration!

CASE 28

DIAGNOSIS: AS

This boy seems to eat a fairly varied diet, including cereal, vegetables, fruit and various meat products. However, he is reluctant to try new things and often wastes food. He has a tendency to bring packed school lunches home untouched.

TIPS

- Sprinkling chocolate over things such as bananas ensures they get eaten.

- Similarly, sprinkling cheese over savoury foods makes them more appealing.

CASE 29

DIAGNOSIS: AS, ADD

This boy refuses most fruit and vegetables but otherwise follows a fairly nutritious diet. He seems to like synthetic fruit flavours, e.g. strawberry milkshakes and orange squash, but won't tolerate the real thing.

TIPS

- To get him to accept vegetables I mash them very finely, gradually making them a little coarser over the years.

- I also make spaghetti bolognese with loads of vegetables disguised in the mixture, or mash things up in a cheese sauce.

- If all else fails, I lie about what things are!

CASE 30

DIAGNOSIS: ASD

This girl ate well as a baby but was difficult to wean off breast feeding. Her mother comments that she would rather starve than eat something she hasn't had before.

TIPS

- Trying to make mealtimes fun by letting our daughter have whatever she wants, usually chips and ice cream, has been very effective in improving her behaviour at mealtimes. She used to refuse to come to the table, or would scream and throw her food away, spit and knock the chairs over. Now she will sit nicely at the table.

- She recently ate chicken again, after a break of several years. We achieved this by giving her breakfast at 7.30, followed by a long walk and no snacks. Lunch was at 1 pm at a friend's house with lots of other children and they all tucked into a chicken meal.

7

More Hints and Tips

As I was going to Banbury,
Upon a summer's day,
My dame had butter, eggs and fruit,
And I had corn and hay
(*circa* 1843)

I made renewed appeals for parents to complete my questionnaires in 2000 and 2001 and the following tips are taken from these. The National Autistic Society (NAS) sent out my details on its website and also printed a notice in its membership magazine which had encouraging results. Sadly, many requests for questionnaires had to be turned down as there would not have been time to process them all. Some of the tips may seem familiar as they are variations on techniques listed elsewhere, but each family added its own unique touches to these strategies, so I feel they are worth reproducing here.

CASE 31

DIAGNOSIS: AUTISTIC

Many of the children in my sample started off eating relatively well, then began to regress around the 18-month mark, as was the case with this young boy. He now eats just six items and five of these are eaten intermittently. Most of the foods he likes fall into the carbohydrate category – plain crisps, white bread, dry Sugar Puffs, Shredded Wheat, chips, chocolate – though he will tolerate a little milk.

TIP

- Will try things in a new setting, e.g. at school, at his nana's, on holiday – these places offer an opportunity to try out new foods.

CASE 32

DIAGNOSIS: AS, DYSPRAXIA

This boy was a very hungry baby but couldn't tolerate the coarser textures of baby food and was frequently sick. He has a general liking for meat, but will not tolerate sauces or gravy on his meals. He also likes curries – the hotter the better.

TIP

- Foods have been reduced to the items he will eat. We give him vitamin supplements to make up for any shortfall in his diet.

CASE 33

DIAGNOSIS: AUTISM

Dietary problems seem to have worsened as this little girl gets older, though she eats a reasonable selection of fruit and vegetables and will eat pasta and some meat and fish products. She has a tendency to 'graze' during the day rather than eat three set meals.

TIPS

- She may try something if it looks similar to something she already likes, e.g. has just started to eat melon, possibly because it looks like apple, one of her staples.

- If she won't eat the food immediately, she may return to it 15 to 20 minutes later and eat, say, cold chips and beans.

CASE 34

DIAGNOSIS: AUTISTIC

This boy has a relatively short list of favourites consisting mainly of foods high in carbohydrate, e.g. cereals, bread, crisps, breadsticks, chips and biscuits.

TIP

- We have no problems getting him to eat…providing it's something he likes!

CASE 35

DIAGNOSIS: HIGH FUNCTIONING AUTISTIC

Dietary problems have been in evidence from the start. He had a milk allergy and was put on a casein-free diet. His favourite foods include plain pasta, baked beans, bread products and potatoes.

TIPS

- Encourage him to be involved in the whole process of food preparation, from buying ingredients in the shop, to opening packets, cooking, serving and then eating the food.

- Videoing him while eating. They did this at school. Then we tried it out ourselves to show the school staff how he was coping at home. His eating behaviour, in general, is much better in the school environment but the process of videoing him seems to improve things at home. Surprisingly, this works even though he doesn't see the end result – he hates to watch himself on video.

- Putting a tiny amount of new food on his plate and giving him lots of praise for just allowing it to be there before actually getting him to try it. Then gradually encouraging him to smell and lick the food without actually eating it. Finally, encouraging him to take a tiny bite.

CASE 36

DIAGNOSIS: AUTISTIC TENDENCIES

Currently on a gluten-free diet, this boy's diet consists of just four foods – Marmite sandwiches, soya yogurt, banana, and white chocolate buttons, though he will take mineral and vitamin supplements. He also exhibits pica, a craving for things not usually eaten, in this case dirt, pink flowers and toothpaste.

TIPS

- He used to eat spaghetti hoops and I would blend meat and vegetables, about the size of an ice cube, into it and he would eat it.

- The 'first and then' method, where you offer the new food and then show the preferred food, had some success. As soon as the new food touched his lips we gave lots of praise, then offered him the preferred option. This required a lot of patience and effort.

CASE 37

DIAGNOSIS: COMMUNICATION DISORDER ON AUTISTIC SPECTRUM

This boy's diet is high in carbohydrates and consists of just five main items – potatoes, plain pasta, cereal, bread crusts and the coatings on crispy foods. On occasions he will try banana and apple.

TIPS

- If his father makes a show of exaggerated pleasure while eating a certain food, my son may try it.

- If you can get something on his lips, with a physical struggle, he will lick it off. He may then go on to eat it. I got him to eat banana in this way.

CASE 38

DIAGNOSIS: AUTISTIC

This boy's main meals consist of cheese pizza, fries, fish fingers or sausage rolls, and he will occasionally try beefburgers. He likes snack foods, including one particular type of iced bun.

TIPS

- We put his favourite toys out on a table at mealtimes and sometimes this encourages him to eat.

- He may try more if he watches children on a video eating. We've taped school programmes showing this and they've been invaluable. They've been used over and over again.

- If he eats his yogurt at school the teacher rewards him by letting him hold her Mickey Mouse watch, or he can wear it for the duration of the meal. Clocks and watches are a current obsession and he is happy to be fed while he has this distraction.

- If he is very hungry, he will sit down and eat food without the need for encouragement. On occasions, if nothing else works, we leave him to eat when he is ready.

CASE 39

DIAGNOSIS: AS, ADHD, DYSPRAXIA

This boy is very sensitive to the texture and smell of foods but he appears to have a fairly balanced diet overall, including some fruits, vegetables, meat products, pasta, potatoes and bread.

TIPS

- To get him to eat meat, I give him very small amounts cut into tiny pieces. I then encourage him to eat by saying 'just two more mouthfuls', etc.

- He will eat pizza if all the 'bits' are removed.

- The promise of dessert is a good carrot to dangle in front of him if I want him to eat more.

CASE 40

DIAGNOSIS: AUTISTIC

This boy has a very limited diet, but he has a liking for taramasalata and hummus dips as a sandwich filling. He will also eat cheese spread, chicken nuggets, fish fingers, toast, salt and vinegar flavoured crisps and KitKats.

TIP

- To widen his diet, we blend fruits and add them to his fruit squash.

CASE 41

DIAGNOSIS: ASD

All but three of the items in this boy's diet are only eaten sometimes. Bread, cereal and milk make up the staples of his daily menu.

TIPS

- Telling him he needs 'decent' food to grow up big and strong makes some impression.
- Letting him choose what he wants from his limited repertoire, so he has what he fancies.
- Distraction techniques, such as letting him watch a video while he eats, can help.

CASE 42

DIAGNOSIS: AUTISM, ASTHMA, ECZEMA, ALLERGIES

This boy eats a vegetarian diet with a reasonable selection of foods, including bread, pasta, cheese, vegetarian sausages and chips, plus several types of dry cereals.

TIPS

- Taking advantage of favourite TV characters as role models, e.g. introducing raw carrots after or while he's watching Tales of Peter Rabbit video.

- Similarly, pretending that a serving of custard was honey while Winnie the Pooh video was on.

CASE 43

DIAGNOSIS: ASD

This boy's difficulties have improved a little over the years and he now eats quite a wide range of vegetables, most types of meat and fish. He follows a gluten-free diet and has soya-based desserts.

TIPS

- The forceful approach, 'try this or you do not watch TV', has some success.

- His own inquisitiveness may prompt him to try something.

CASE 44

DIAGNOSIS: AUTISTIC

There have been some improvement in this boy's basic diet over time. He now eats a choice of cereals, bread, pizza, sausages, fish fingers, pizza and a range of snacks.

TIPS

- Buying similar foods with a slight difference and letting him try a little at a time has helped in introducing new foods.

- Being able to reason more as he gets older e.g. explaining that different packaging on products does not mean that the food itself has changed. He is also able to tell us what he likes and dislikes now, before this he would simply go without food unless we happened to give him something he liked.

CASE 45

DIAGNOSIS: AUTISTIC

This teenage boy's diet consists of a small number of familiar foods. However, he will now have milk on his cereal, formerly it had to be dry, and recently tried his first plain burger at McDonald's. Prior to this he had never eaten a sandwich of any description.

TIP

- If we don't pressure him, he sometimes tries things his friends suggest. I don't know whether he enjoys them, or if he thinks he is pleasing somebody he respects.

CASE 46

DIAGNOSIS: AUTISTIC

At 16 weeks old this boy suffered an anaphylactic shock reaction to a rusk product and has subsequently had adverse reactions to various foods, which restrict his diet even more. He eats a range of cereals but is very influenced by product types and packaging. He will eat one specific type of beefburger, plus pasta, dry toast and a range of snacks.

TIPS

- I keep old cereal boxes and when the design changes I put the new cereal in them without his knowledge.

- He has a preference for certain shapes. If his toast is shaped to his liking he will eat it; if it isn't, he won't.

CASE 47

DIAGNOSIS: AUTISM

Diet problems first started around the 18-month stage when he restricted his intake to chicken dippers, chips, peanut butter on toast, apples and fromage frais. Three years on, the diet is much the same, though the fromage frais is now out of favour. He also likes a selection of snack foods.

TIP

- The headmaster at his school came up with this tip which has worked with other fussy eaters. You take a Hula Hoop snack and place small bits of different foods in the middle, letting the child watch you do this, so they are aware they will be expected to try something different. The process can be slow. It may need to be repeated daily for up to three months before the child will try it. This strategy was recently tried out on a little boy who would only eat Hula Hoops and sweets. Now he eats everything on the school dinner menu.

CASE 48

DIAGNOSIS: ASD

Some foods, such as yogurts, are thought to make this young boy hyper-active, so they've been taken out of his limited diet. He is very brand specific but will eat certain types of sausages, burgers, ham and chips.

TIPS

- To get my son to eat burger, sausages, chips, etc., I let him get used to one taste at a time. We allow around a week on each, for example, two burgers one week, chips another, then sausages, then we put them all together as a meal.

- He has a need to be occupied while he's eating, otherwise he won't sit still for long.

CASE 49

DIAGNOSIS: ASD

The family of this young boy see his problems as being worse now than when he was younger. He eats lots of carbohydrates but will also try sausages, cheese spread and yogurt.

TIP

- As he seems to lack a motivation to eat, it can help physically to put food in his hand or even into his mouth.

This is most successful when he is distracted by something else, e.g. looking at a book.

CASE 50

DIAGNOSIS: AS

This boy's diet is almost exclusively carbohydrate based though he will tolerate cheese on pizza. He eats cereals, toast, biscuits, crisps, chips, bread and pasta, but draws the line at eating fruit and vegetables, with the exception of the occasional apple.

TIPS

- The least fuss you make over trying new things, the better the result. We try and keep the pressure off at mealtimes. He may accept new foods on his plate while informing us that he won't be eating them. We reply that this is fine, as it increases his tolerance of more foods.

- He used to refuse anything with turkey in it, but he has a great interest in dinosaurs and will now eat turkey dinosaurs because of this.

CASE 51

DIAGNOSIS: ASD, COMMUNICATION PROBLEMS

In common with several other boys in this sample, his dietary problems became apparent around the age of 18 months, and his parents feel things have worsened in the meantime. He will tolerate some fruits but has a particular liking for bread, crumpets, malt loaf and cereal. Chicken dippers, fish fingers, sausages and chips are also currently in favour.

TIP

- The old chestnut of smelling a food before progressing to licking it, then tolerating it in his mouth has had some success. We added the proviso that he should hold it there for a count of ten. If this is successful, he then moves on to swallowing it. We offer him something he likes as a reward if he manages this.

CASE 52

DIAGNOSIS: AS

Although there are relatively few items in this boy's menu, they all seem fairly nutritious. He'll tolerate some fruit and vegetables, potato, pasta, toast, yogurt, meat and fish products.

TIP

- The sneaky approach – we'll encourage him by saying 'just four more spoonfuls', then start counting and pretend to forget what number we've got up to, so we have to start all over again. This typically gets at least three more spoonfuls in and makes eating fun.

CASE 53

DIAGNOSIS: AUTISTIC

There are nine foods on this young boy's preferred menu and eight of them are high in carbohydrates. In common with many other children in the sample, he will eat chicken in the form of nuggets.

TIP

- Providing our son with his own table and chair has been quite successful. He becomes distressed if made to sit at the big table and will eat more when he is on his own.

CASE 54

DIAGNOSIS: AS

Among the usual preferences for bread, cereal and pasta, this boy lists chicken masala curry as a favourite. He also likes steak, gammon, ice-cream and various snacks and treats, including chocolate cake. As a toddler he ate a fairly varied diet, but things have worsened since starting school.

TIPS

- Telling lies can help. For example, the mashed carrots aren't carrots at all, it's just that the potatoes are a bit of an orangey colour today.

- He is currently in a class one year up from his age range. Since he hated the younger class, we tell him that if he doesn't eat he will be too small for his present class and will have to go back to the old one. This encourages him to eat on some occasions.

CASE 55

DIAGNOSIS: ASD

There are 11 familiar items on this little girl's menu, but in common with many others, she'll only eat them some of the time. When she's in new surroundings, e.g. away from home or on holiday, she may go on hunger strike for several days.

TIPS

- When my daughter refuses to eat, I don't try to force her any more. Instead, I take the pressure off either by taking her plate away, or by concentrating on my food and telling her how nice it tastes. I try to minimise anxiety by keeping calm myself.

- It sometimes helps if she can look in a mirror or at a picture of herself while she is eating.

- I also tell her that the food she is eating is one her favourite character likes, e.g. 'this spaghetti is like Barney eats'. This has had some success.

CASE 56

DIAGNOSIS: ASD, HYPERACTIVITY

Another young boy whose problems were first apparent around the 18-month mark, his problems are seen as getting worse over the years.

He has quite a rigid diet consisting of cereal, chipolata sausages, pasta, tuna and toast. He will eat apples, oranges, strawberries and melon, but also has a liking for sweets and white chocolate spread on his toast.

TIPS

- Trial and error – experimenting with different food brands to find one he likes and keeping a food diary to record any successes.

- Using props such as cocktail sticks, funny shaped dishes and bright coloured plastic cutlery to gain his interest.

- Spreading out a travelling rug and having a picnic on the living room floor to make mealtimes fun.

Summary

When we're given a list of strategies to try, all of us feel hopeful that maybe there's a magic ingredient in there that will be successful with our child. In many cases, there will be a successful outcome with some suggestions, but the nature of this intolerance means that what may be a spectacular success on Monday may be a dismal failure on Tuesday. One lesson I've learnt from my own experiences is that you simply have to try and try; even if you seem to be getting nowhere, try again. Having said that, we can all relate to the sense of frustration felt by the mother of this young AS boy who survives on just four items of food of dubious nutritional value. In the tips section of my questionnaire, she penned the following:

A mother's lament

We make eating into a game, turning the food into imaginary Ford, Vauxhall and BMW cars, but the novelty wears off after one or two mouthfuls.

We give lots of praise and encouragement, to no avail.

We ignore him completely at mealtimes, hoping he will get hungry and want to be included, but he never gets hungry.

We set a *special* place for him at the dining table, but he won't sit still for 30 seconds.

We buy novelty foods to tie in with special interests but he doesn't want to eat them, he'd rather play with them instead.

My trump card? Banging my head against the wall in despair!

On a more optimistic note, I've weeded out a selection of tips which seem to have rated particularly well in the success stakes. There's no harm in putting them to the test.

TOP TEN TIPS

1. Be persistent. Even if your child has rejected a new food on several occasions, keep trying. It might just become familiar enough to be tolerated one day.

2. Structure is all important to autistic children. Aim to have regular mealtimes and cut down on snacking, where possible. Although hunger levels can be unpredictable among these children, coming to the table with a relatively empty stomach is always preferable to trying new foods when they're satiated from a snacking session.

3. Excessive amounts of liquids between meals will fill up a child so much that they won't want, or need, much food. Try to cut down on too many drinks throughout the day.

4. Don't overload your child's sensory equipment by offering a plateful of food, or a mish-mash of ingredients all jumbled

together. Think small and keep different foods in separate areas of the plate if your child prefers this.

5. Never force feeding issues. Take the pressure off by letting your child simply sniff or look at foods in the early stages of feeding programmes.

6. Try to make mealtimes fun (see the recipe for creating a Splodge in Chapter 12). Aim to get your child accustomed to the feel and smell of food without the pressure of having to eat it.

7. Experiment with a little reverse psychology, i.e. if you ask ASD children to do something, they probably won't, so tell them they can't possibly have a peach, artichoke, melon segments, or whatever, as it's only for grown-ups and quite unsuitable for children. Curiosity might just get the better of them.

8. Don't rule out reward strategies, offering preferred food for trying something new, or working with your child's obsessions – in fact try anything that has a positive element and works.

9. If your child has a preference for crunchy textures, add cereal toppings, grated chocolate or fragments of crisps to food to make it more appealing.

10. Try to empathise with your child's fears. He or she isn't deliberately being awkward by refusing food and changes are unlikely to happen overnight. Take the softly, softly route. There's a good chance that we'll all get there in the end.

8

What We Think of Food

If all the world were paper,
And all the sea were ink,
If all the trees were bread and cheese,
What should we have to drink?
(*circa* 1641)

An interview with Ros Blackburn

Ros is well known on the autistic circuit as a very entertaining speaker with forthright views. As well as battling with autism, she also had to cope with a fear and dislike of many foods in her childhood. Now aged 32, she still follows a restricted diet, but things have definitely improved over the years.

Q: Have you always had eating problems?

A: Oh yes, right from the start. I think in many ways my mother was sad for me because I was missing out on so much. I would say, 'Oh I don't like whatever,' and she would point out, 'But you haven't even tried it.' Some of these things were considered to be luxuries, but I was too scared to try them. My mother didn't mind my not liking a few things, because everybody has things they don't like, but I had such a limited list of things that were acceptable.

Q: What things did you eat?

A: I liked typical children's food. Fishfingers and chips, sausages and chips, baked beans and lots of tomato ketchup. The sort of things that whole generations of little Britons have grown up on.

Q: And things you disliked?

A: I remember strawberries was one, and peaches another, oh and cream. My mother would say, 'Just try a little bit,' and I would get the most minuscule amount, not enough to give it a chance really, and say 'No, yuk, yuk.' My mother would say, 'How do you know you don't like it when you haven't even tried it?' But I was actually terrified of the food, terrified of trying it.

Q: So there was a real element of fear where food was concerned?

A: Yes, definitely. It was terror with me. I was terrified of the feeling, and the fear of the unknown of the taste, everything to do with eating. I was worried about…not just what it would *taste* like, but what it would *feel* like in my mouth, and I think even now it is the texture of a lot of food that puts me off. And smell is another thing. Cinnamon is something I will not go near even now, because the smell is so revolting. I was also scared of the noise food made in my head.

Q: Noise is a new one to me. Is that very important?

A: Well, I love crisps but some brands are too crunchy, and the sound is too over-powering in my head, so I avoid them. I prefer one particular brand of plain crisps to anything else. They're not too brittle. It's sound and texture, as well as flavour that's important.

Q: Were you influenced by the colour of food?

A: I don't like food that doesn't look 'natural', but that's just a quirk. I mean, I wouldn't like my food to come up bright pink or bright red, or bright yellow or something, but it doesn't really bother me.

Q: What about 'new, improved recipes', were they a problem?

A: Yes, that was a nightmare. I would end up hanging on to the last old one if they brought out a new version. For example, I used to love one kind of meatballs. Then they changed the recipe and I bought the new sort and they were hideous so I scoured the shops to get as many of the tins of the old version as I could. I ate them all, except for one, and now the one remaining tin is going to go out of date and I'll probably have to throw it away. It's happened with so many products and, more often than not, the new version is never as good as the original. I don't know whether it really isn't as good, or whether it's just that I don't like change. It might be that the new meatballs were not as nice but then, gradually, I suppose, you forget what the old ones were like and you get content with the new.

Q: Do you have a preference for hot or cold foods?

A: I don't like my food to be too hot. I can't taste it when it's too hot. I used to cook things until they were lukewarm and my mother wasn't happy because she said it wasn't safe. Now, if I go out to eat I have to wait until the food cools down. I could never see the logic of why people spend extra time and money cooking meals hot, then waiting for them to cool down, when you could cook them half hot in the first place.

Q: Many autistic children seem to like predominantly plain foods. Is that the case with you?

A: Definitely, yes, I do like bland things. People say 'oh, it's so boring', because I tend to play safe. I'd never, ever, go into the realms of the totally unknown. As a child I seemed to have totally irrational rules that certain foods were okay and others weren't. Things like shepherd's pie, or cottage pie with mashed potato on top were a complete no-go. The strange thing was there was nothing I disliked about minced meat or mashed potato, but put the two together and it was a horrible combination.

Q: What do you dislike about the texture of food?

A: I prefer plain versions of most things. I mean, I will eat plain fairy cakes if my mum cooks them, and I will eat sultanas raw out of the jar, but if she cooks currant buns I don't like them.

Q: Why is a currant bun so awful?

A: It's the texture. When you bite through the bready bit, and then suddenly squish into the currants. You can *hear* it as well, as you squish into the currant you get a noise in your mouth. Some of these fruity things have almost got a gritty noise and a feeling that's *foul*.

Q: Do you dislike food with 'bits' in general?

A: Yes, even to this day I have to have smooth yogurt with no bits in and marmalade with no bits. I think it's the contrast of textures in my mouth I object to. For instance, if you're eating strawberry jam and there's pieces of fruit in it, it has a squishy feel. It's unexpected and sudden and makes me feel out of control.

Q: Did lumpy textures make you afraid of choking?

A: Yes, sometimes, with certain foods. Meat was one. I would chew and chew for hours on end, and I was terrified of the lumps in mashed potato and custard. It was the fear of suddenly encountering a lump, the fear of feeling a lump on your tongue. I was also worried about swallowing pills. Even today I can't do that. I worry that one will get half stuck in my throat. As a child, my dad would crush them between spoonfuls of lemon curd so I could swallow them. Now I crunch them in my mouth and then gulp water.

Q: What other foods are currently on your Ugh! list?

A: Anything that changes consistency once it's cooked. For example, I will eat a raw apple, but if you cook an apple and make apple pie, I will not eat it because it gets the most hideous smell to it, and the most hideous texture, and the most hideous taste.

Q: If you dislike food, does it go straight in the bin?

A: Absolutely not. Quite often I make myself ill by eating everything on my plate and it adds to the anxiety of getting something I don't like because I can't leave it. People say, 'Oh just leave what you don't like, it's all right.' But I can't and that makes me really anxious. I am really specific about having, say, just two pieces of something or three potatoes and five and a half runner beans because I just can't waste anything.

Q: Have you ever really liked a food then suddenly gone off it?

A: I think I've gone off foods gradually, and then I've tried them again later on. I used to love ginger beer with ice-cream melted into it. In the summer I'd get home from school and have some and it was a real treat. I had to be a good girl for ages just to merit one of those. When I was living on my own I suddenly thought I'm going to have ginger beer and ice-cream, but I didn't like it. I think I don't like sweet things as much as I used to. I tend to prefer savoury things now.

Q: Have you made a conscious decision to opt for healthier foods as you've got older?

A: Absolutely not. I still adore crisps and chips but I do like things like leeks and courgettes now. I have massive gut problems but I don't do anything about it. If I were to go on a gluten-free or casein-free diet I've been told I would feel considerably better inside, but I adore pasta and bread and chocolate, so I would be as miserable as sin. My behaviour might improve, but then again do I care whether people are on the receiving end of my obnoxious behaviour or not? Other people might benefit if I went on a special diet but I don't care about that. I don't want to suffer by not eating what I like.

Q: Why do you think some autistic children like certain foods at home and others, say, only in a restaurant or at school?

A: Because it's familiar. It's a rule, an obsession, a routine. It creates order and lets them stay in control. I think for the person with autism in general, the real world is so totally incomprehensible that they need to cling on to a certain amount of structure and routine in their lives. They want to have a time when they are in control and this is very much the case with me.

Q: Have things generally got better as you've got older?

A: They've improved somewhat. I still live off chips. I can eat chips any time of the day or night, but I will try some new things now. For instance, I like strawberries now and also peaches and grapes, all things I used to hate.

Q: What do you think brought about this change?

A: My mum and dad's perseverance. They would give me something I liked, say a plate of chips, and something I didn't such as a tea-spoonful of shepherd's pie. I wasn't allowed to get down from the table and play or do something I really wanted if I didn't eat the shepherd's pie. I had to sit there. Once they'd started on a strategy, they never, ever backed down, even if I had a huge tantrum and they ended up getting attacked or whatever. In those days, I'd eat the chips first, then agonise over the shepherd's pie for hours. Nowadays, I'll start with the nasty thing first, gulp it down with water, think, yuk, I don't like it, and then get on with enjoying the plate of chips.

Q: What age were you when things started to improve?

A: I think around 11 or 12 when I went to a boarding school. There were still lots of things I didn't like to eat, but the rules were that we had to try a little of everything. Now, on the whole, I adore food and I would love to be able to go out to restaurants, but I can't because I have little support and if I go on my own I get silly comments made about my being a young girl eating by herself.

Q: So your parents' techniques seemed to have worked?

A: Yes, I suppose it was a form of behaviour modification. Things like not allowing me to get down from the table and play or whatever affected me a great deal. It wouldn't work for everyone but it worked for me. I think children with autism learn differently because they're not motivated by social priorities.

Q: Can you expand on that?

A: At the end of the day the non-autistic is motivated to conform because of their desire to get on in society, they want to have social acceptance. They might be worried about making a fool of themselves, for example, at a formal dinner, whether they're using the right cutlery, etc., so that motivates them to learn the correct way to do something. But I don't get embarrassed. I don't care what people think. You would have to tap into something that really matters to me to get results, such as my passions and obsessions.

Q: But what about the child or adult with AS? They crave social acceptance too.

A: The rules are totally different for them. I don't even know why children with autism and Asperger's syndrome are lumped together. If you were to say to a child with Asperger's syndrome 'mummy will be upset if you don't try a little of that', it might work because the child wants to please. However, it wouldn't work at all with me because I don't care what effect my behaviour has on other people. I wouldn't care whether mummy was happy, sad or indifferent.

Q: But as a general rule, tapping into the interests of children on the autistic spectrum seems to get results?

A: It does for me, definitely. Not just for eating disorders but for managing behaviour in general. I mean, it's highly controversial because you are modifying the behaviour of a child, bribing, whatever you want to call it.

Q: And your advice in a nutshell?

A: Never, never make autism an excuse but help the person overcome the problems caused by it. Try and motivate these children by finding out what matters to them. If their passion is the half-an-hour that they're allowed on the computer, then try banning it until the food is eaten. They have to eat a tiny bit, it doesn't have to be much. Be reasonable. Maybe a teaspoonful to start with, just tiny, tiny bits, one mouthful, then build it up to two mouthfuls and so on. I am so glad my parents did that for me.

Why I don't like food

It's all very well asking doctors, dieticians and psychologists why our children won't eat, but for a real understanding of the problem, it makes sense to consult the experts. I asked some children with autism and AS what it was about food that they disliked or feared. Some of them even told me what they liked:

> I don't like food because it tastes horrible. I don't like bread or anything like that because sometimes when I'm eating it, it feels horrible and so I spit it out. Then I look at it and that makes me feel sick. Last time that happened I was sick for real. The reason why some food smells nice and I don't try it is because I don't think it would have a nice taste when it's in my mouth. I don't like drinking, or having left-over bits of milk because I only like the taste of it on my cereal. I don't like 'bits' because they look horrible and I don't like the new KFC ketchup because it tastes too healthy and I don't like healthy things a lot, I'm not a fan of them. I don't like trying new things because I'm not used to them and I don't want to get used to them. (Harry Legge, 11)

Autistic children can take things literally, so the phrase 'apples blow you up' can be quite terrifying. My friend, also autistic, has never eaten an apple because of this, and if anyone is seen eating an apple, can become quite distressed. The media [advertisements] can be confusing and cause upset. Why would anyone dare to eat chicken dippers if they make people's mouths go all stretchy and crazy, and then the house starts to dance? This is frightening until insight into our own autism is gained. Graphic portrayals of people breathing fire after eating spicy foods [another advertisement] are equally disturbing to autistic children, so why *would* they want to eat it? I wouldn't. My friend had many food phobias that made him *appear* to be very stubborn but now, after guidance, he is coming out of it, and is also discovering that exploding chocolate with misleading jingles really can be eaten for fun. I once had a phobia of drinking because it aggravated the sensory imbalance, resulting in toilet visits, which I was always being punished for at school. My solution was, don't drink, and I became quite dehydrated because of the school's ignorance of autism. Another problem is taste *distortion*, due to the sensory imbalance. It's not always easy to judge taste or even tell if food is safe, because taste is not always identifiable to us. (Anon)

Sometimes I feel that it takes too much time to eat, and it disturbs me when I am playing out with my friends. (Alexander Sumner, 8)

I don't like the taste and texture of some foods. I wouldn't want to try beetroot…just thinking that it's a plant and eating plants is horrible, I don't like the look of it and I don't like sprouts. I tried spaghetti bolognese once, even though I didn't like the way it looked. I actually quite liked it. I only tried a tiny bit, but I don't usually have it now. I like some meats, but not real meat like lamb. I like dinosaur ham [a type of luncheon meat]. I also like cucumber and peppers, and raw carrots. Raw things are crunchy. I like fruit too, but sometimes it is not all that sweet. If there are strawberries I would eat them. I like sweet things, and things that are very concentrated. I like biscuits and sweets but potatoes are ugh! The texture of potatoes isn't nice but I like chips because they are fried and are salty. I like sweet and sour sauces from McDonald's but I don't like ketchup because I hate tomatoes. Cheese and tomato pizza is all right. It sounds a bit silly because I don't like tomato but I don't like any other toppings, things like pepperoni, I don't like the feel of them. My favourite food is strawberries, they are really yummy if you put sugar on them. They look nice, they smell nice, they taste nice and I like the shape. They feel a bit like carrots, but softer. I like fizziness in drinks, like Lucozade, not things like spring water though, they need to be sweet. (John Copeland, 12)

Eating is one of my biggest difficulties. I can't explain why I have this difficulty, but for me this is the worst thing about AS. The thing I absolutely hate most is trying anything new. There are hardly any foods I eat at all. I especially hate any foods with bits in it, or things mixed together with each other, like cheese mixed with bread in a cheese sandwich, or mixed colours of foods. Sometimes I can eat a bit better if I am left on my own…I don't like to eat any food which is the wrong texture…Most food has a horrible texture. Like mashed potato for example…It feels like papier maché which might go into every crevice of my mouth like a sculpture. (Kenneth Hall, 11. Taken from Kenneth's book, *Asperger Syndrome, the Universe and Everything.* 2001, pp.46-7)

Kenneth also told me:

I hate the texture and taste of onions and Brussels sprouts. Pringles are my favourite food. I like the way they look, and taste, and the colour, smell, and texture of them. Pringles and chocolate make me happy. Bits are horrible. In soup, for example, you might find a bit which is a small lump which irritates you, and you just don't like it.

I don't like vegetables because they taste awful, and have a crunchy texture. I don't like fruit that much, most kinds, but I don't mind apple crumble because the apple is boiled and squishy. My favourite food is Chinese – ribs, prawn balls, most things. Some things I just don't like the taste of. I don't like toasted cheese sandwiches because the cheese doesn't taste nice after it's warmed up. I don't like fruit cake because of the fruit. I once tried it and stopped eating it because I didn't like the taste. (Paul, 16)

I don't like cake because I think it makes me sick. My favourite food is chocolate crispy cake (home-made with cooking chocolate and Rice Krispies). I only like them if they're melted. They're the only cake I like. I like chocolate. I wouldn't want to try new foods because they might make me sick. I think that chocolate crispy cakes are the best food. I only like crunchy things. At birthdays I have a cake and I make a wish and blow out the candles but I never try it. I once had a tiny crumb of birthday cake but it made me feel sick. (Rachel Scowcroft, 6)

The black and green bits [of food] look like they are bad for you. They are scary and take the skin off you. (Russell Coates, 5)

Pasta doesn't taste of anything. I don't like meat because it tastes different to other meat [he only likes sausages]. I don't like garlic bread because garlic is spicy and it's bad for you. I don't like pizza because it doesn't have any topping on that I like. I don't like cheese because it's too milky and it's only for mice. (Nicholas Bastiman, 11)

I like sweets because you can suck them, chocolate because it melts, and caramel because of its stickiness. I don't like Brussels sprouts because they have a horrible taste. Foods that are golden yellow are the best. I don't like the bits in yogurt but don't mind them in jam. I wouldn't try food if it was smelly or coloured brown or green that I didn't know, I need to know what it is first. The smell gives a clue as to whether food is good. If some bits are black that's a clue to its being bad. I don't like fizzy drinks because they are tangy. I like apple pie and sausage. (Christine Gregory, 7)

Toffee and fudge are my favourite foods because they taste nice. Smell is important. I want to try nice-smelling foods but I would not like to try food that smells unpleasant. I taste food I don't know by touching it with my tongue. I hate Brussels sprouts and mange tout. I also think Sugar Puffs stink. I really like pasta and toffee, they are my favourite foods, not together though. (Robert Gregory, 8)

I don't like Italian food, and things with meat or fish and…I don't know what else. I just don't like these things. Texture is very important but I don't know why. My favourite foods are Indian, Chinese and Aunt Bessie's vegetarian toad in the hole, moussecake [cheesecake], home-made garlicky bread, Hovis country grain bread, toasted and home-made vegetarian sausage rolls, sausage and mash and carrots with vegetable gravy, sliced potatoes casseroled in stock and nutburgers dipped in milk because they are tasty. (Anon)

Some foods taste yucky – yogurt stinks like dog poo, it gives me a headache. I like beefburgers – they have peas on the box, there are no peas in the box. I like to eat by myself. I don't want to sit at the table. I don't eat food because I am not hungry. (Jack Mawbey, 6)

Some foods are disgusting. (Samuel Bennett, 7)

I don't like eating meat as I always feel like I'm eating a dead animal. I feel like the blood's inside. I only like white bread because brown bread is disgusting. (Leon Elkan, 9)

I don't like the smell and texture, bits and seeds. A lot I've tried but can't stomach. Even being near vegetables makes me feel sick. A lot of soups and things have too many different things in them. (Benjamin Smith, 16)

I look at it, and I am not sure what is in it. (Carl Major, 7)

The reason I don't eat new foods is that previous experiences of tasting new foods weren't enjoyable. So, it's basically stick with what you know you like. I don't like soggy or slimy foods. (William Schofield, 15)

I don't like the smell or feel of some foods. (Paul Charlesworth, 4)

But you know what I like [as told to his mum]. I like sausages and chips. Why do I have to eat vegetables? They're yuk. (Matthew Charlesworth, 10)

I don't like some foods, and most people don't like some foods. It's a stupid question. (James Charlesworth, 12)

Many of the children surveyed found it extremely difficult to talk about food dislikes and likes and I was reluctant to press them in case I put them off the few foods they could tolerate. Others were physically unable to talk or write down their feelings, so the sample is much smaller than I had originally hoped for. However, the difficulty of this exercise makes the accounts of the children who did respond all the more remarkable. As noted in other sections of the book, there is no such thing as a typical child with classic autism or AS — they are all unique. Some seem to eat quite a wide variety of foods, whereas others are locked into eating just one or two things. However, all the children in this sample are perceived as having food intolerances and many of the difficulties seem to be related to a heightened sensitivity towards food and the eating environment in general. The look, smell, sound, taste, colour and feel of certain foods can be enough to render the most desirable dish of the day inedible to an autistic child. Their views are invaluable in helping us to understand the confusing world of autism, and perhaps the comments above will help us to empathise a little more when our children show fear or distaste at mealtimes.

9

Social Difficulties

This little pig went to market,
This little pig stayed at home,
This little pig had roast beef,
This little pig had none,
And this little pig cried, wee-wee-wee-wee-wee,
I can't find my way home.
(*circa* 1728)

Coping with our culinarily-challenged children at home is one thing, but letting them out into the big wide world is something else entirely. If the world doesn't appear to be ready for children on the autistic spectrum yet, it certainly isn't ready for children on the autistic spectrum who won't eat.

It's party time
We first realised social occasions might be a tad difficult when Harry's first birthday came around. It wasn't a party as such, but I'd invited neighbours and family round and slaved away to provide a suitable spread, dominated by a rather flat, home-made sponge cake. There was jelly too, and bite-sized sandwiches, sausage rolls, crisps, chipolatas and animal-shaped choccy bikkies, plus fruit juice, fizzy pop and hot drinks for the grown-ups. Quite a feast if I say it myself. Most of the food was

Harry tucking in to all the food we'd have liked him to eat on his fifth birthday (Cartoon courtesy of Frank Dickens)

eaten, but not by the birthday boy. Harry ate the princely sum of a handful of crisps, one chipolata and two animal biscuits.

This pattern was repeated on subsequent birthdays, but his cavalier attitude to food drew even more attention when he began to get invitations to other children's parties. Most children turn up at parties with a card and present for the child at the centre of the celebrations. Harry also came with a carrier bag containing a selection of the few foods he would eat, plus a bottle of diluted orange squash. Now if anything is going to upset the hostess, it's the arrival of a child carrying a moveable feast. The more you try to protest that it's perfectly natural for your child to decline every item on the party table, the worse the situation

becomes. The more paranoid partygivers will think that it's either (a) a
hygiene issue or (b) a reflection on their ability to make edible sandwiches. Invariably they find it impossible to comprehend that there
won't be a single item on the menu that he'll tolerate. Consequently,
they'll add little extras to his plate as the afternoon wears on – the odd
sausage here, a couple of sandwiches there, a tiny vol-au-vent and some
of the crisps his mother said he wouldn't eat, because everybody likes
them. Unfortunately, if any of these new items touch any of the familiar
ones on his plate, the likelihood is that nothing will get eaten.

It's even worse when the hostess goes out of her way to be helpful:
'Tell me what he likes and I'll get some in.' Because you don't want your
child to be labelled a complete eccentric and because you hate to put
people out, you vaguely mention that he likes chicken nuggets, without
specifying that he'll only eat one brand from a particular supermarket
which doesn't have any local branches. On the day, he's presented with
a plate of 20 chicken nuggets, the like of which he's never encountered
before and which he fervently hopes he'll never encounter again. As

*Do people really eat this stuff? It's enough to ruin a good birthday. (Harry with his
    friends Ayla and Michael)*

they're being offloaded into her pedal bin the hostess makes a mental note (1) never to believe a word his mother says; and (2) to make sure he's not invited to her next jamboree.

The very laid-back party hostesses are no better. I once delivered Harry to a sports hall for an event which was to be followed by a meal. My protestations that 'he can be difficult in that department' were met by cries of 'oh don't worry, we'll find something he likes'. When I collected him a couple of hours later, she seemed a trifle less accommodating. Having failed to find a single item on the party menu that he liked, she'd marched him off to a vending machine and invited him to choose whatever he fancied from its extensive selection of crisps and chocolate bars. Moreover, he could take his pick of drinks from the adjoining machine to wash it down. Needless to say, his current favourites weren't on offer in either machine and, to add insult to injury, he didn't like the contents of his party bag either.

Of course, I'm making the assumption that children with ASD get invited to parties in the first place – very often they don't. As Gunilla Gerland (1997, p.40), a young woman with high-functioning autism, points out: 'I didn't realise that parties were a result of having friends, and that you had friends by playing with other children. It wasn't contact with other children that I missed, but parties meant cream cake. I also wanted some cream cake. I wanted to go to parties and be given a bag of sweets.' She goes on to say: 'On my birthdays, when I was to have a party, children seldom came because I didn't know any.' In that respect, we were quite fortunate. Harry had a small nucleus of friends from early childhood who invited him to a number of parties over the years, despite his obvious lack of interest in the catering arrangements. Contrary to the impression given above, Gunilla also fell into the category of a very picky eater in her youth. Earlier in her book she confesses that 'I had no need for variety in my food. I just liked eating the same things all the time…for long periods I ate nothing but skinless sausages and chocolate pudding' (Gerland 1997, p.14).

When it came to Harry's turn to throw a party, we had fewer options than most families. His idea of the ultimate feast was to invite his friends to McDonald's, Burger King or KFC. The first time it was quite a novelty, but when his friends began to receive their fourth and fifth invitations to a fast food party some of the surprise element had gone. It didn't help that the timing of his fourth birthday party had coincided with the incubation period for a bout of chicken pox. We had thought he was a little quieter than usual on the day, but were horrified when he came out in a blotchy rash the following morning. His social standing plummeted to new depths when we had to phone round all his friends, ostensibly to enquire if they'd enjoyed the party, but more crucially to discover if they'd come out in spots yet. Some of the more sensitive ones declined the invitation to his next party.

A meal out

If you regard meals out as leisurely occasions to be enjoyed, you don't have a child with eating intolerances in the family. In fairness, things are a lot better for us now, but early visits to eateries were fraught with tension. No matter how extensive the establishment's menu, the likelihood of finding a single item our son would like was as remote as encountering an igloo in the desert. Consequently, we either fed him first or dangled the promise of a Happy Meal before him as we tucked into our own meal. You can imagine how it appeared to other diners. Two adults filling their faces with a three-course meal, while their child sat contemplating an empty place setting. Even worse, if he hadn't eaten first, he'd be complaining in a loud voice that he was hungry and enquiring whether it would be long before he could eat. The waitress would invariably ask what the child was having, just in case we'd forgotten him, and there were often loud comments from other tables about our non-existent parenting skills.

Mind you, things weren't much better on the occasions he did join in. The obligatory knife and fork were always rejected in favour of fingers and the chef's special was soon reduced to a unappetising mush as the search for 'bits' got under way. Moreover, our assurances that 'everything is fine' and 'yes, we are enjoying our meal' sounded pretty hollow when Harry handed back a plate containing a pile of discarded batter, all the green and black bits from his chips and the portion of baked beans we'd repeatedly said he didn't want, but which they'd decided to give him anyway.

Some establishments are undoubtedly better than others at coping with the unusual demands of faddy children. An employee at one local department store couldn't have been more helpful when I asked her to improvise a bit with a standard kid's menu. As we were in a hurry, I asked if animal shapes and chips could be purchased as a takeaway. No problem. And could you leave off the beans or peas because he won't eat them? No problem. And because he isn't having a side dish, could he have an extra animal shape? No problem. And could he have a diet coke in a cup, because he doesn't like drinks in a carton? Slight problem – the choice was between a glass, which couldn't be taken away, or a carton which could. However, as a compromise, we were given a cardboard cup without a protective top, as they didn't stock them. Now, that's what I call service!

At least we have the option of eating out as a family occasionally. For some families this is virtually impossible. Two of the children in my sample would only eat off the floor, literally, without the niceties of crockery to streamline the process. Apart from the embarrassment factor for the families concerned, it might be difficult to find a chef who was willing to dish up his speciality on a well-scrubbed bit of cushioned vinyl. Another family were wary of eating out when their child was small: 'He would be sick if anybody was eating anything that he could smell nearby. He used to sit at a table on his own, and we could never order anything with a garnish as he would start to vomit and cause a scene.'

Other children would reduce their limited food intake even more if they were taken out for a meal. One mother said, 'She will only eat *one* food off the plate when we go out, e.g. only chips or pasta, even if there are other things there that she likes. This has been getting gradually worse, and she is really only comfortable eating at home or in a familiar environment. If I encourage her to try things while we are out, she usually has a tantrum and gets very upset.'

Sometimes families have given me a fresh insight into things I thought I already understood. For instance, I assumed that the general reluctance to use cutlery by some autistic children might be due to poor co-ordination or difficulties with fine motor control. However, one young adult with AS still eschews cutlery and avoids other people who eat with a knife and fork simply because he hates the noise they make. Several children have reported that they actually need to feel food before they eat it to determine whether the texture is acceptable. All perfectly logical, but try explaining these things to fellow diners and other family members who are convinced your offspring should have grown out of these 'childish behaviours' by now.

Then there's the difficulty of actually deciding what to eat, as ASD children are notoriously bad at making decisions. If your child likes two or more things on the menu, the process is particularly painful. Ros Blackburn told me about the problems she faced when eating out: 'When I get the menu I just cannot decide what I want, and I'm scared of making the wrong choice.' Other factors come into play too. For Ros, eating out is a special treat that happens rarely so there's a great onus on her to get things right first time. 'I worry about food wastage, and also the waste of an opportunity to go out to eat. Going out for a meal may be a once a year kind of thing and therefore there's a lot of pressure on me to get it right, to get a meal that I will really enjoy.'

On occasions, the only way to ensure that there will be something acceptable on the menu is to take your own food in. Some establishments get a bit precious if you do this, but sometimes it's the only solution to a very trying problem. For instance, your child might like one item on a restaurant's menu but none of their beverages. In this event, do you:

(a)   order the meal without a drink, or

(b)   risk upsetting the rest of the clientele by whipping a made-up bottle of economy squash out of your Save-It carrier bag?

Similarly, if you are keen to eat together as a family, would you:

(a)   risk being branded a cheapskate by retrieving junior's portion from the depths of your handbag and placing it in full view of fellow diners, or

(b)   ask him to eat his package of food surreptitiously (preferably under the table) and away from prying eyes?

Some mothers have become old hands at coping in this situation: 'I often take my own food when we're eating out and, without anybody noticing, slip him a bread roll. He generally has that and refuses to eat the rest. Sometimes people look at you, but I live in hope that he'll be a bit more flexible as he gets older.'

Even the simple matter of eating chips can become stressful when your child insists on following a set routine at mealtimes: 'My son must dip each chip into ketchup. He bites into it, then the remaining chip is 'spent', i.e. no longer fit for consumption. When he was younger, he would dispose of this portion by projecting it, at considerable speed, across the room.' The parents concerned have since resolved the issue by employing TEACCH[1] work station methods to deal with the problem. Now he has a plate with chips on his left, a small plate with ketchup in the middle and an empty plate (for spent chips) on the right. However, his mother still has the occasional hiccup in some establishments when serving staff query the need for extra plates: 'One or two have been rude, but I suspect they would have been rude in the face of any request above and beyond what was usual and expected.' She went on to say, 'Perhaps the biggest problem was my own embarrassment and fear of asking for extra plates.'

The less formal environment of fast food establishments can give rise to a fresh set of problems if your child is hypersensitive to noise and large gatherings. 'If Burger King is too crowded, he won't go in,' con-

---

1   TEACCH stands for Treatment and Education of Autistic and Related Communication Handicapped Children. It was Introduced by Eric Schopler of the University of North Carolina, USA in the early 1970s. The program aims to help people with autism to cope at home, school and in society by reducing or eradicating autistic behaviours.

fessed another mother. 'If we do manage to persuade him, he will go and sit at a table on his own, and cover his ears if the music is too loud. Usually, we have to ask for it to be turned down, or off.'

Fast food menus have to be modified to meet the specific tastes of other young diners. One little girl is very particular about the number of McDonald's chicken nuggets she will eat. 'She always has to have ten of them and will only eat the outsides of them,' her mother told me. Since nuggets are typically served in fours (with Happy Meals), sixes, nines or twenties, this added to the expense of eating out. Moreover, it was a bit of a pointless exercise anyway as 'she always leaves two of the ten, regardless of hunger levels'.

The holiday season

Forget the sun, sea and scenery. If we're off on holiday the main criterion is whether or not our destination has an acceptable fast food establishment nearby or at the very least a decent chippy, which is why we eschewed the local pleasures of wine tasting, admiring fields of poppies and cycling on a family holiday to Burgundy in favour of dining out in the nearest McDonald's. In case you need to know, it's just down the road, in Dijon. Of course we did try to acclimatise Harry's palate to brioche, croissants, local cheeses and coq-au-vin, but the excellence of French cuisine continues to remain a mystery to him, whereas he can appreciate the unique attributes of American fast food joints.

Of course it is possible to take enough food with you to see you through a week or, heaven forbid, a fortnight's holiday. This strategy doesn't leave a lot of room for other essentials such as clothes and makes a mockery of the concept of 'travelling light', but it's sometimes the only solution on offer. However, in deference to the added restrictions brought in with the recent foot and mouth disease scare, it might be advisable to stay put if your child has a fetish for meat and dairy products.

If your child likes typically British products, going abroad can be a nightmare. One family's visit to Canada was marred by the fact that they typically sell fresh fruit juices there and not the concentrated squash variety. Since junior would only drink orange squash and the family had exhausted the limited supply they'd brought with them, the race was on to find a suitable replacement. 'We thought we'd packed enough, but it was gone in no time. When we ran out, everyone began to panic.' By the time they'd come across a specialist shop selling British products, including Marmite and, joy of joys, orange squash, their boy was showing early signs of the delirium associated with extreme dehydration. No matter that the shop was charging approximately double the cost of the same product at home, it was considered a small price to pay for rehydrating their son.

Holidays are rarely a relaxing time for the mothers of faddy eaters. Self-catering outlets are invariably the preferred option, which means that a large part of the holiday is taken up with buying, preparing and cooking food to their child's unique preference. Unlike the package holidaymaker, who knows if it's Monday it must be Portugal, the harassed mum catering for her picky child hasn't a clue what day of the week it is since she'll probably be serving up the same dish from Monday to Sunday – of course, that's assuming that the child will eat at all. The pressure of dining in a new environment can be enough to make a picky eater go on hunger strike. The mother of one 7-year-old girl on the autistic spectrum who had a very meagre diet to start with said, 'She eats very little anyway, but if we go away from home, she can go for days without eating.' On balance, we're probably all better off staying at home.

10

Exclusion Diets

A little old man of Derby,
How do you think he served me?
He took away my bread and cheese,
And that is how he served me.
(*circa* 1815)

When our children have behavioural problems, we want to do everything in our power to help them and, if we're honest, ourselves. Given the choice of a child who has perfect manners and won't show you up in public and one who is likely to have a major tantrum at the busiest checkout in Marks & Spencer, we'd all plump for the former. So when tangible evidence suggests a link between diet and poor behaviour in children on the autistic spectrum, we all start pricking our ears up.

Gluten- and casein-free (GF/CF) diets

The basic premise is that some children on the autistic spectrum are unable to digest various proteins satisfactorily – the chief offenders being grain products such as rye and wheat, which contain gluten, and milk and dairy products, containing casein. It's suggested that these poorly digested proteins may adversely affect brain function and removing them from the diet of susceptible children should result in a significant improvement in behaviour and general health.

That's the good news. The bad news is that when your child is on a very restricted diet to start with, the implementation of a GF/CF diet is well nigh impossible. For instance, were I to remove all items containing these two proteins from my son's diet, he'd be surviving on fresh air. The experts on diet will tut knowingly at this information. According to them, my child is craving the very things that do him most harm. All I have to do is remove them and, at best, I'll have a completely different and healthier specimen on my hands. At worst, I'll have a corpse.

Tests and implementation

Before introducing a GF/CF diet it's vitally important to find out whether your child has an intolerance or not. Although a sensitivity to gluten is thought to be one of the most common food intolerances, it can be difficult to detect accurately, and shouldn't be confused with a wheat *allergy* which is relatively rare. Wheat allergies can give rise to problems like eczema, nettle rash and asthma. Wheat *sensitivity* is more difficult to diagnose and thought to cause symptoms such as hyperactivity in children and behavioural problems similar to those induced by narcotics.

The proteins mentioned above form peptides, which are believed to enter the bloodstream via a 'leaky' gut. These peptides can be measured by a special urine test. Dr Paul Shattock at Sunderland University uses a high performance liquid chromatographic (HPLC) test to establish the presence of peptides in urine, which are then plotted on a graph. If the results show a significant level of peptides, it's arguable that a GF/CF diet might be worth trying. There are also blood tests which can identify the problem, but no test can offer conclusive proof that your child will benefit from this type of diet. The British Nutrition Foundation argues that in some cases what appears to be a wheat intolerance may be purely psychological.

If you wish to act on positive test results, an elimination diet is the next stage, but this should only be undertaken with a lot of support and guidance from a dietician. The standard procedure is to cut out foods containing gluten or casein for a trial period of three to four weeks, then to reintroduce them gradually and check for behavioural changes. One problem is that a great many foods contain gluten and it can be very hard to eliminate without imposing a very restrictive diet. One mother compromised by putting her son on a low rather than a no gluten diet because the former proved too difficult to follow: 'Even when we thought everything was out of his diet, there were still tiny traces in other things, and…to be honest, I couldn't see any significant behavioural differences when he was on the no-gluten diet.' To complicate matters, even so-called gluten-free foods may contain wheat. Of the two proteins, casein is thought to be simpler to exclude and some people try cutting this out first.

In *Special Diets for Special Kids*, Lisa Lewis reports how her autistic son's behaviour improved within days of excluding wheat from his diet: 'Sam's aggressions dropped dramatically, and I began receiving wonderful reports from school' (Lewis 1998, p.13). However, she admits at the outset that 'I am lucky. Sam is not a fussy eater and accepts the various substitutes I provide for him'. She acknowledges that this diet would be very difficult to implement if children eat few foods to start with: 'Making a radical dietary change will be very traumatic for these families, and it is just common sense to determine whether a GF/CF diet is likely to help before proceeding' (Lewis 1998, p.51).

Indeed, that brings us to the heart of the matter. Is it possible, or even advisable, to try to put your child on such a diet when they have severe eating intolerances to start with? Or are we merely being wimps if we decide that such a regime isn't for us? The parents I spoke to were divided on this subject. Many of them had given it a go, then realised it was too difficult to implement and returned to the original diet. Others couldn't even contemplate trying it because their son or daughter only ate two or three foods already. A third group was full of praise for a GF/CF diet and would wholeheartedly recommend it to others.

This diet can be especially difficult to follow when there are other children in the family who are still eating conventional foods. One mother had this to say on the subject:

My son has been on a gluten-free diet for eight months now. It's fairly difficult to implement, and there have been a number of blips. My other children like chicken nuggets, but the only time I can cook them is when he's at after-school club. On one occasion they hadn't eaten them all, so I put some out for the dog. Before I knew it, my son had found them and was eating them out of the dog's bowl.

However, the rewards for following the new diet may outweigh the disadvantages: 'When he's had gluten he becomes quite emotional... he will cry and easily get upset about things...his behaviour has definitely improved in some ways.'

For others, the diet is too restrictive to implement: 'My son lives off sandwiches, yogurt and cereal. Cutting them out would require a major overhaul of his diet. If I was at home all day, I could possibly cope with it but it just seems like some mountain that I can't face climbing.' Nonetheless, she did give the diet a trial: 'I tried to remove milk by replacing it with soya, but he spat it out and we had a temper tantrum. It just made life so difficult. I also tried a rice bread and that met with the same reaction. I suppose we fell at the first fence.'

When you meet opposition from your child at mealtimes on a daily basis, trying out a new diet can be fraught with difficulties. My own view, for what it's worth, is that the diet is an excellent one and has a lot to recommend it if your child is receptive to trying new things – and that is a very big if. For parents of children who are extremely selective eaters, it's a completely different ballgame, and none of us should feel guilty if (a) we daren't try it or (b) we've attempted it and failed. If people have never had to deal with a child who has a very restricted diet, it isn't really possible to identify with the sheer helplessness we can feel when our children refuse to eat. Of 29 items itemised in a list of acceptable foods for those on a GF/CF diet, I was only able to tick five that Harry would possibly try – potato chips (and he may not like the taste of the type he was allowed), fruit (certain types only), poultry, fish (cod only) and potato.

> I often hear from parents whose children eat only four foods, typically chicken McNuggets, French fries, pizza and milk. You may find it difficult to believe, but a GF/CF diet *is* possible for such a child (Lewis 1998, p.65)

The book goes on to list a wide variety of recipes which offer GF/CF alternatives to these favourites. However, if your child has highly developed senses, he or she certainly won't be fooled by a healthy alternative to familiar foodstuffs. It's a bit like the fairy story about the princess and the pea. No matter how many mattresses were placed on top of the offending pea, the genuine princess was always acutely aware of its presence and would toss and turn all night. It wouldn't have mattered a jot whether it was a petit pois or a thumping great chipshop pea, she would still have been able to detect it. Similarly, no matter how skilfully you dress up a healthy food to resemble a fast food favourite, it's a virtual certainty that your child will be able to suss it out. The stark fact remains that GF/CF foods do taste different to the old favourites and for some children this is one hurdle they simply can't get over. The mother of one autistic boy said: 'We've tried a few gluten-free products and he just turns his nose up at them, so I was kind of trying to introduce the new food before withdrawing the old, so it would be a gradual process but he wouldn't even touch it. He sticks with what he knows basically.'

Another parent told me: 'We did a gluten-free diet for a short while. It was horrendous because he would hardly eat anything and he wouldn't try any gluten-free bread, no gluten-free biscuits, and he was continually hungry. He didn't have any energy and was very low.'

Not only do the new products need to have an acceptable taste but they also have to meet all the criteria that make familiar foods appealing. The mother of a 5-year-old boy diagnosed with an autistic spectrum disorder said: 'We're trying a GF/CF diet at present but it is hard to find substitutes that have the same texture, taste, and look that he will eat on a regular basis.'

In some cases there's a danger that introducing new foods might put children off one of the few items they will currently tolerate. One little girl in my sample would only eat cooking chocolate, chocolate biscuits, a specific type of yogurt, Wotsits and milk. The parents had attended a lecture on GF/CF diets and were advised to try her on a mixture of 50 per cent rice milk mixed in with the normal version until she adjusted to the new taste. But as her father pointed out: 'The big worry was that she'd stop drinking fresh milk.' Since she had rejected other foods that had once been in favour, there was good foundation for these fears:

> At one time she used to eat Cadbury's chocolate buttons, then someone bought her another brand and we knew there was no way she would eat them. It was decided to put the new buttons in a Cadbury's packet so they'd look familiar. Not only would she not eat them, but she's never eaten buttons again. If you start messing about with things they will eat it's a big gamble...if she cut fresh milk out we would be in big trouble.

The introduction of new tastes also proved difficult for another family:

> When I tried to get him used to rice milk by adding a very small amount to a glass of cow's milk he wouldn't go near it as he said it smelt "stinking". He goes mad when his brother is having rice cakes or soya produce and says they smell so bad that he can't stay in the same room.

Why not give it a go?

To listen to some exponents of alternative diets, you'd think that parents who won't consider them are fearful stick-in-the-muds whose aversion to change can only be bad news for their child. I would suggest the opposite. Ultimately, we're all doing our best in a very difficult situation. If there was a cast-iron guarantee that our children would accept the healthier food substitutes we'd all be delighted to experiment with them. But there is a risk factor involved and there could be serious consequences if it all went wrong. If a new diet would distress our children or make them even more unhappy about food in general, is it worth taking the risk?

One young autistic boy with a history of vomiting and poor eating patterns has had regular visits to his local paediatric gastrology clinic over the years. His mother says this about GF/CF diets:

> My son does not fit the typical profile of the autistic child with gut problems who would benefit from a GF/CF diet. He has had very few infections or illnesses and has *never* had an antibiotic, I couldn't get them down him. [Antibiotics are thought to be a possible causal factor of damaged intestines.] A specialist asked us if his behaviour, interaction, eye contact, etc. were better when he ate less, i.e. an unintentional reduction in gluten intake, and we reported that the phases when he eats less tend to coincide with a deterioration in all round behaviour and interaction.
>
> Although I have always tried to be open minded and supportive about the GF/CF diet and associated theories, I find that I am becoming more and more exasperated by the pressure put on others by those parents following this path. I do believe that there are some children who definitely suffer from gut problems and who benefit from this type of diet, and supplements etc., but I think that these theories are getting a little out of hand and being taken *far* too seriously by *far* too many people. Some parents are becoming fanatics with no acceptance that there is genuinely a case for not following their path.

If parents have attempted the diet for a trial period, then later abandoned it, there's always the nagging suspicion that maybe it wasn't carried out thoroughly enough in the first place. Perhaps if more foods had been excluded, more small print read on dubious packages, more care taken in preparing meals, there might have been a better result. But even when the diet is followed to the letter, there are no certainties that it will make a great difference. Anna Parton, the dietician whose interview appears in Chapter 12, decided to try her son on the diet:

> I had my son tested by Dr Paul Shattock and his graph showed a peak, so I opted to try him on the gluten-free diet for six months. I decided I was going to do it 100 per cent properly but I can't say that we saw any massive improvements.

However, she remains supportive of the diet:

> In my experience, having seen quite a lot of children who have embarked on these diets, I would always recommend that people have a go, where possible. It's always worth trying out. The children who are helped by the diet seem to be turned around very quickly, and in these cases the impetus to stick to the diet is there because the child suddenly starts talking, making eye contact, or whatever. Then they may start eating a bigger range of foods so the initial worry of restricting the diet goes away. But the fact remains that it doesn't help everyone. I think it's most important for the children who have lots of ear infections and upper respiratory problems in early life, the ones who've had to miss school. They're the ones that tend to suggest there might be problems. Although it didn't necessarily help my son, I'm still quite open to the whole intolerance/allergy thing.

Anna recalled one mother who had managed to put her son on a GF/CF diet successfully, but she had the benefit of a supportive family. When the new regime was first introduced there were lots of teething troubles:

> The child didn't eat anything for two weeks and his mother had two weeks of no sleep, two weeks of tantrums. Then he started eating, but those two weeks were the longest of her whole life, and he needed a lot of support from me. I take my hat off to her because I don't know whether I would have been able to do it, but she didn't have any other children, wasn't working, and had support from her family. All those things are really important. If you're on your own in a flat with two other children around you, well it's not going to be easy.

It helped me

When any type of intervention is successful, it encourages and inspires the rest of us, even though it may not be a regime we could implement ourselves. The following accounts show that a GF/CF diet can work given the right circumstances. David [name changed to protect identity] is a 44-year-old man with long-standing diet problems, diagnosed with AS and paranoid schizophrenia. His dietary preferences are largely determined by how various foodstuffs make him feel, with things like taste, texture, appearance and smell relegated to second, third, fourth and fifth places respectively. At 19 years of age he went on hunger strike and lost a lot of weight. Later, he heard about exclusion diets and decided to give a GF/CF diet a try:

> I felt much better without wheat and dairy products in my diet. Having been a vegetarian since I was a teenager, on and off, it was easy to replace foods without me becoming upset in any way. There is just a bland taste in the diet I'm on now, but the only thing I miss is the taste and smell of cheese. The diet has made a definite improvement to the way I feel and think. My behaviour has changed for the better, and there are no more voices and visions. I would recommend this diet to anyone.

Colin Revell, 38, is another advocate of a GF/CF diet. As well as AS, he also has to contend with dyspraxia, ADD and dyslexia. However, unlike most of the people I spoke to, Colin has always eaten a wide range of foods, so it wasn't too traumatic to experiment with new tastes and textures, though he found the GF diet rather bland:

> I used to eat a lot of junk food, and craved for things with gluten in, like burgers, kebabs and chips. Then I read about GF/CF diets and the work of Paul Shattock on the internet, and decided to try it. I've been on the diet now for about two years but it's been difficult.

Colin has had quite a few relapses in this time and given in to cravings for pizzas and chocolate, but always tries to revert back to a GF/CF diet following these blips. 'When I follow the diet I seem to get calmer, more responsive, I don't get into conflict as much, and my obsessive compulsive behaviours improve.' Physically, Colin noted that problems with tonsillitis and sleep apnoea seemed less prevalent when he modified his diet. Some improvements were evident within days of starting the new diet and were noted by professionals involved in Colin's care, but it has been a constant battle to keep to the fairly strict regime.

As well as gluten and casein, Colin also tries to cut out salicylates (a natural chemical substance found in fruits like apples, berries, grapes, plums, oranges, cherries and tomatoes) and caffeine. He describes coming off his old diet as like 'coming off a drug. You have withdrawal effects, like cold turkey, and my body craves gluten'. Despite all the setbacks, Colin remains supportive of his new diet:

> All my family have suffered from gastroentrological problems. I think it's a good diet but the sooner you start the better. Once you're an adult, it's so much harder to give up gluten...I turn back to the old diet when I'm frustrated with myself. It's a kind of self-harm for me. When I eat food with gluten I feel better at first but then my stomach starts to bloat, I get hyperactive and my symptoms in general just get worse.

However, his main bugbear is the cost of the new diet:

> I know that my old diet caused me a lot of damage. I should have the right to buy GF food in the supermarket at the same price as other foods. It's a human rights issue that should be addressed.

11

Doctors and Dentists

I do not like thee, Doctor Fell,
The reason why I cannot tell;
But this I know, and know full well,
I do not like thee, Doctor Fell.
(*circa* mid-1600s*)*

As long as our children remain healthy on their limited diets, we can fool ourselves that the problem is perfectly manageable. However, when illness strikes it can add a whole new dimension to things. In fairness, the children are not deliberately being obstinate patients when they refuse to take sustenance or medication at this time, just remaining true to an intolerance that is neatly summed up in the medical directive 'nil by mouth'.

When Harry first experienced high temperatures and childhood bugs, he was going through his 'strawberry phase', so we were able to administer Calpol, a paracetamol suspension, and Cefaclor, a straw-berry-flavoured antibiotic, without too many problems. The doctor may have thought I was a bit peculiar when I always insisted on the strawberry version of whatever was available, but he was willing to humour me. However, around the age of six or seven, Harry decided that he'd had quite enough of Calpol and never wanted another spoonful of the stuff to pass his lips. So when he contracted tonsillitis and had a series of raging temperatures, we could do little to ease his discomfort. Since the illness also made his food 'taste funny', we suffered a double whammy and had to watch helplessly as he refused all food and his usual medication for a period of ten days. However, some good did come out of this. We resorted to paracetamol suppositories as a means of reducing his temperature and his loathing of taking anything by mouth meant that he was much more willing to accept this type of medication. Staff at the local hospital used a spot of child psychology to encourage him to eat, but this was less successful. 'If you don't eat, son, we'll have to have you in hospital.' one doctor told him. However, such was his terror of eating that a hospital stay sounded positively peachy by comparison. 'When can I go into hospital?' he asked, convinced that this was the lesser of two evils. Towards the end of his fast, we discovered that he'd lost around 4 kg in weight and pleaded for him to be put on the waiting list for a paediatric feeding clinic, as a matter of some urgency. We finally got an appointment several months later, by which time his illness was a distant memory and he had reverted to his limited diet once more.

Doctor's orders

When the illness is preferable to the cure, parents are faced with a very difficult dilemma. We can sweeten the pill by crushing up tablets and dissolving them in juice, but most pills have a very bitter taste and can easily be identified by a pernickety patient. One mum admitted, 'I put a threadworm tablet into a drink of Ribena last year and he has not touched Ribena since, although it used to be his favourite drink.' On the other hand, these children seem to have quite high pain thresholds and don't appear to be unduly concerned by the things that alarm most other young patients. The mother of a 12-year-old boy with AS said: 'He has never taken tablets or medicine, and I don't know what we would do if he were really ill. When he was four, and had to have his booster injections and oral polio drops, he had the injections without a sound, but screamed so long and loud at the polio drops that all the surgery staff came out to see what was wrong!'

If a child has a fear of gagging, pills and capsules must seem terrifying. The standard advice is to split open capsules and mix the contents with something acceptable. Similarly, tablets should be crushed to a powder and dealt with the same way. However, although this deals with the problem of bulk, children with hypersensitivity to different tastes may still be reluctant to take their medicine.

Dr Christopher Green could empathise with this difficulty: 'Doctors have no difficulty in writing prescriptions for children, the problem comes when it is time to force the foreign substance down the toddler's firmly shut trap.' Remedies he suggested included asking for 'a more palatable alternative' if a medication had been refused in the past, or requesting a drug that could be administered, say, twice a day instead of four times, to lessen the agony. With liquid preparations, it's recommended that the unwanted substance is quickly followed by a gulp of a favourite drink. Alternatively, the contents could be transferred to a needleless syringe and squirted into the mouth – the fun element of this has a lot to recommend it. Other tactics Dr Green suggests, which might also appease ASD children, include hiding small tablets in a portion of ice-cream and making a sweet mini sandwich, consisting of a thin layer of ice-cream on a teaspoon, followed by a crushed tablet, with a topping of jam or chocolate (Green 1984, pp.186-7).

Half the battle has been won if your child has a liking for a particular flavour as some medicines come in options such as banana, blackcurrant and strawberry to appeal to kids. However, a pharmacist I consulted pointed out that it isn't a good idea to keep specifying the same type of antibiotic as it could lessen its efficacy. If time were no object, we could ask to have an antibiotic, for example, made up in a specific flavour, but it takes around ten days for manufacturers to produce a tailor-made medicine, by which time, presumably, the child would no longer need it.

Steps we can take

1. Don't sit back quietly as your doctor writes out a prescription. Point out that your child prefers some flavours to others. Always ask if there are alternatives.

2. Your local pharmacist is another useful contact. Pop into the chemist and explain that your child is reluctant to take medication. He or she will have a good idea of what is available and may be able to recommend something that is relatively inoffensive to take.

3. Never consider using any medicine without prior medical advice.

Did you know?

1. The drug Ritalin, which is often prescribed for children with ADD and ADHD, can act as an appetite suppressant.

2. Low levels of zinc in the diet may also result in a poor appetite.

Vitamins and minerals

Ideally, children should get all the vitamins and minerals they need from a comprehensive diet, but if your child were on an adequate diet, presumably you wouldn't be reading this. If you're concerned that your son or daughter's food intake is inadequate, it makes sense to get them professionally assessed by a dietician. Coming up with our own ideas about what pills or potions they may be lacking could be positively dangerous.

When Harry's food intake was first assessed, by submitting a record of what he had eaten over a five-day period, our dietician concluded that he was receiving 68 per cent of the recommended normal intake of calories for a boy of his age. However, he was not meeting the lower recommended intake for calcium, folate or B12. The good news was that he was meeting all the other vitamin and mineral lower recommended normal intakes, despite his very restricted diet. To redress the balance, he was prescribed Sandoz, a colourless calcium syrup that could be mixed with drinks, which he accepted happily, plus multivitamin drops with a disgusting smell, which he wouldn't tolerate. Only by speaking to other mothers with similarly pernickety offspring have I discovered less offensive alternatives. Approach your doctor or dietician for a consultation if you think any of these preparations might be suitable for your child. The supplements tolerated by children in my 'picky eaters' sample (their inclusion here is not a recommendation) are as follows:

- Calcium-Sandoz – clear syrup with a fairly inoffensive taste

- Sandocal effervescent calcium tablets

- Paediatric Seravit – a vitamin and mineral supplement in powder form, available in unflavoured and pineapple versions

- Dalivit oral vitamin drops

- Boots multivitamins – chewable strawberry flavour

- Junior Forceval – vitamin and mineral supplement in capsule form

- Paracetamol suppositories

- Fortifresh nutritional supplement with vitamins, minerals and trace elements, gluten free, available in blackcurrant, mandarin and raspberry flavours, not suitable for very young children.

- Scandishake – for conditions requiring fortification with a fat/carbohydrate supplement – comes in powder form to be mixed with milk, available in chocolate, strawberry and vanilla flavours.

If you want a brief description of commonly prescribed medicines, for example to find out whether more palatable flavours exist, you can consult the British National Formulary, which should be available in the reference section of your library. Alternatively, take a look at *www.emc.vhn.net*, which offers comprehensive information about hundreds of pills and medicines. Set up by the Association of the British Pharmaceutical Industry (ABPI), the service allows patients to make informed decisions about medication for themselves and family members. Only products of companies affiliated to the ABPI are included.

Supplementing diets

The best way to receive vitamins and minerals is through a diet rich in fruit and vegetables. Ironically, these are probably two of the areas of highest food refusal among picky eaters. Recommendations that our schoolchildren should eat five fruit portions a day to ward off illnesses such as heart disease won't make a jot of difference if we can't get them to eat. If your children like flavonoid-rich fruits (the good guys) such as apples, blackcurrants, cherries, oranges, lemons, tomatoes and plums, congratulations. Similarly, if they'll eat beetroot, cabbage, carrots, lentils, cauliflower, lettuce, peas, parsley, spinach, watercress and potatoes, take that self-satisfied smirk off your face! The rest of us may have to get in the queue for supplements.

Calcium deficiencies

Although it was alarming to discover that Harry's diet was lacking in calcium, it was also gratifying to realise we could do something about it. The earlier deficiencies are discovered, the better, but it's never too late to improve poor dietary habits. A big concern was that brittle bone disease or osteoporosis might occur if the status quo had been allowed to continue. His intake of cereal, milk and ice-cream products have helped to increase dramatically the amount of calcium he receives from food, but it's comforting to know that there is an alternative should his dietary habits change.

Dental appointments

Many children and adults have a fear of going to the dentist. Worries about painful tooth extractions, the noise of the drill and concerns about injections in a sensitive area are all things we can readily identify with. However, if your child is on the autistic spectrum and has food intolerances, their worries are likely to be of a far more nebulous kind. Will they have to have a horrid tasting gel in their mouths? Will they have to rinse out with that strange, pink-coloured water? Will the mixture for fillings taste awful? Pain seems to be very much a secondary consideration. The real dread is of encountering something new and unpredictable and it can take a very special kind of dentist to understand those fears.

Harry's sweet tooth has resulted in a number of visits to dental surgeries. At one point, we thought that the best solution would be to consult a special needs dentist, in the belief that professionals in this area would show more care and compassion in treating him. However, the term special needs covers a very wide area and there are no guarantees that these dentists will understand the peculiarities of children on the autistic spectrum any better than the usual variety.

There were crossed wires when Harry turned up for his second appointment with a special needs practitioner. 'Have you done this before?' he enquired nervously as the dentist tried to place some paste in his mouth, meaning 'is this a new experience for me?' or 'have I had this taste sensation before?' The dentist, however, took the query as a slight on her credentials and snapped back, 'Of course I've done this before. I'm a qualified dentist!'

Things went from bad to worse when it was suggested that Harry should use disclosing tablets to show up plaque, so he could improve his skills with a toothbrush. At first he was very reluctant to use the tablets, but when he discovered they were red and didn't taste too bad, we were able to make some headway. We were thrilled with his progress, but the dentist was less than impressed. 'The red tablets aren't so good,' she informed a nonplussed Harry. 'What you need is some nice *green* food colouring. Put it on with a cotton wool bud. That will really show up the plaque.' Needless to say, this is not the best way to deal with a child who has an aversion to putting anything new in his mouth. At least we have had some success with dental hygiene. Other families haven't been so fortunate.

> He won't use disclosing tablets because he says he couldn't possibly put anything like that in his mouth, and if I make too much of a thing of him brushing his teeth, he really rebels. He doesn't like being reminded that it's important to make sure his teeth are really clean.

The real dilemma arises when the few foods our children will tolerate are of the sweet and sugary variety. If we impose a total ban on sweet things, we may have solved the problem of dental caries, but we're left with a gaping hole in their menus. Our rather unsympathetic dentist asked us simply to remove most of the chocolate from Harry's diet, though she was willing to allow him a sweet treat with his Friday meal. Suggestions as to how we should do this, or what we could replace it with, fell on deaf ears. Another mother told me:

> He has problems with his teeth because I can't get him off sugary biscuits and I don't know what else I can give him. I'm not deliberately going out and buying them but giving them as a last resort, in desperation really, because he won't eat anything else.

As caring parents, we can hardly condone a diet that damages our children's teeth and results in lots of stressful visits to the dentist, but making overnight changes to diet can be well-nigh impossible. The long-term aim should be to wean our children onto a healthier diet, but there are some tactics we can try out in the meantime.

1. Ask your dentist about protective coatings which are painted onto the biting surface of adult teeth. Known as fissure sealants, these coatings make it easier to maintain dental hygiene and help to prevent decay.

2. Try to minimise the amount of sugary snacks your child eats throughout the day. If sweet treats are eaten immediately after a meal, they are thought to cause less damage. This is because the saliva produced at this time helps to keep teeth clean, so there's less likelihood of plaque being formed.

3. If your child likes cheese, encourage him or her to nibble on a cube half an hour before or after indulging in sweet foods. It's believed to cut down the amount of harmful acid produced. Milk has the same effect.

4. If you can't wean your children off chocolate, try to steer them towards low-sugar varieties – dark chocolate with a low fat content is preferable.

5. Nothing can compensate for good dental hygiene. Try to encourage children to brush teeth well morning and night (I know it's not easy). If they have a sweet snack and it's not practical to clean teeth afterwards, get them into the habit of having a glass of water afterwards to wash sugary deposits off precious tooth enamel.

If you're fortunate enough to find a good dentist, half the battle is won. Word of mouth is probably the best way of finding the right practitioner, so if your friends speak highly of someone, see if you can get on their list. Currently we all see the same family dentist, who has no special needs qualifications but knows exactly how to put Harry at ease. Before doing any work, he explains what is involved, using a mirror if necessary, to show Harry the area he'll be working on. He also takes time to explain the necessity for good dental hygiene. His assistant always chats to Harry and rewards him with a choice of stickers after the treatment. As a consequence, Harry no longer dreads his six-monthly dental visits, but accepts them as a necessary routine. Another mum told me this about her experiences with dentists:

> In the past, we've had horrific experiences with our son when he had to have dental work done. The worst times were before we realised he was autistic. On one occasion he had to have two extractions and four fillings. It took four adults to pin him down, one on each limb, before sleeping gas could be administered. Then, surprise, surprise, he never wanted to step foot into a dentist's again. It took almost three years to persuade him to go back, when he badly needed a filling. I didn't want him to have another general anaesthetic and eventually, after loads of work and preparation, he sat in the chair and had his filling done with no pain relief or anything. It really wasn't the pain that bothered him, or the drill, it was the intrusion – the fact that he didn't trust that person to stick a hand in his mouth.

However, the story has a happy ending:

> I've found a fantastic dentist now, who has five children herself. She broke him in very gently. For two years we'd just turn up and stand at her door, and she'd simply wave at him, then we'd go away. It's all about giving them lots and lots of control, I think that is what really helps to build their confidence.

If you're interested in gentle approaches to this problem, holistic dentistry might appeal. Here, the emphasis is on prevention rather than cure and amalgam (metal) fillings are not typically used, rather homeopathic and herbal remedies are the norm.

You can find out about holistic dentists in your area by visiting the British Homeopathic Dental Organisation's website on *www.bhda.org,* or click on the link to holistic dentistry on *www.postivehealth.com* for more information. Another useful site is *www.bite.uk.com.* Here dentists give advice on how to avoid and cope with tooth erosion, as opposed to tooth decay. Tooth erosion occurs when teeth are attacked by acidic substances such as those found in fizzy drinks and fruit juices. If children must consume these drinks, it's recommended that they shouldn't brush teeth immediately afterwards, as tooth enamel is at its most fragile then. You can find out more about tooth decay, which is defined as the localised effect of damage by acids in the mouth feeding on carbohydrates, by clicking on the British Dental Association (BDA) website link.

12

Professional Advice

Little Tommy Tucker
Sings for his supper,
What shall we give him?
White bread and butter.
(*circa* 1607)

Coping with dietary disorders can be a very isolating experience, and all of us wish we could give a list of our grievances to an expert and be offered a foolproof method of rectifying the problem. More often than not, we come away from long-awaited medical appointments feeling more disillusioned than ever. Sometimes the expert seems to be as bemused by the problem as we are, though few would admit it, which is why I was particularly delighted to discover a dietician with an extra qualification that made her eminently able to advise on this topic. Anna Parton is the mother of a six-year-old autistic boy who was an extremely fussy eater. Anna isn't offering a miracle cure but, having experienced the problem at first hand, is able to draw on this knowledge to help others.

Q: When did you first notice the problem in your son?

A: I would say around 15 to 18 months. At first he ate vegetables, purées and all those sorts of things, but when the diet became more restricted I could probably count the foods he would eat on the fingers of one hand. He would have diluted blackcurrant juice, chicken nuggets, oven chips and chocolate cereal, but only specific brands. That was pretty much it. That was my base line, so it wasn't really the most extensive of diets.

Q: Had you encountered many children like your son in the course of your work?

A: I've been a dietician now for 20 years and in my whole career I think I'd probably seen two autistic children before I had my son. Whereas I was speaking to a paediatric dietician the other day and she estimates she sees around three a month. I don't know whether that means there is greater awareness now, or whether there are more children with the problem.

Q: Do you think the advice you were giving out formerly would help an autistic child, or do they need fresh methods?

A: I think they need a different approach. In fact I've done training sessions to the paediatric dieticians at my local hospital because we aren't just dealing with a straight faddy eating problem here. You can apply the same sort of rules to some extent but I think you have extra sensory, perceptual, visual and textural problems to deal with that don't affect 'normal' children.

Q: Is it difficult to educate others about the special needs of these children?

A: I've very much made it my mission to make dieticians that I have contact with more aware of these problems. It isn't easy. You and I can have a good idea of what something tastes and feels like in our mouths but it might have a completely different taste and texture to an autistic child, and it might be different again between two autistic children.

Q: So each autistic child is, in effect, a unique case?

A: Definitely. I think I've never met two autistic children or two AS children who were the same. Every single one seems to be different and I think it's really important that people respect that. Rather than making assumptions, I try to really find out what the problem is with each individual, whether it's the texture, the taste, or the look of food that's particularly important. I remember one autistic teenager who said that anything crunchy felt like eating barbed wire, so she couldn't bear to have anything with that texture in her mouth. It felt like her mouth was being cut to shreds.

Q: What advice would you offer to mothers of autistic children with eating problems?

A: I think the big message is to have a really positive and persistent attitude. My son has got the stubbornness of an ox and can really dig his heels in, but I decided he was going to eat a bigger range of foods. I was realistic and knew it might take some time but whether it took a week or three weeks (in reality it took about two years to extend his diet), I was going to keep plugging away at it. On many occasions I would present him with food and he wouldn't eat it, but I wouldn't stop presenting it. That's the most important thing really, keep on giving it to them, keep on and on…and try to make it a really positive and fun experience.

Q: Isn't that easier said than done?

A: Yes, you need to be quite inventive. We did a lot of playing with food, making potato prints, looking at food, chopping food, burying food, growing food, and my big breakthrough with my son was making something called a Splodge, which I still do with him every now and again. Basically, this is making a huge 'concoction' with every single item you've got in your food cupboard and just letting him pour it into a bowl in one big heap. Then he could smell and sniff it. I know it sounds disgusting but it was a means of actually getting him to try and put new items in his mouth. That was the biggest thing because he wouldn't even taste something new, he wouldn't even put it near his mouth.

Q: How did you achieve that?

A: Sometimes we would get a grape or a bean or whatever it was that we were putting into this big mix and let him put it in the bowl by spitting it in. Most psychologists and educationalists would probably have a seizure about it, but it was just a way of showing him that food was not as awful as he thought it was going to be. We weren't asking him to eat it, we were just playing and experimenting with food. It was very successful because once he had actually got these foods in his mouth and had a vague taste, he realised they weren't so horrible. On occasions, a few weeks down the line, he would say, 'Can I try some of that?'

Q: What else can parents try?

A: I used to put things in the middle of the table rather than on his plate. I did this with my elder son as well, because he also had some eating problems. The idea was to have whatever family food we were having in the centre, plus some of the food that I knew my children would eat – in other words, familiar foods in among some new stuff. Then people simply helped themselves. To introduce more of a fun element, my kids often liked to make scenes with their food – faces, or boats, or farmyards or whatever.

Q: Was snacking a problem?

A: I wouldn't allow him to snack too much in between meals. If he was a bit hungry he'd be more inclined to try something new. If he cried and moaned and had hysterics, well, I'd know I wasn't starving him. He was going to have his dinner, but as a grown-up I'd made a few choices for him, and I chose for him not to eat chocolate in between meals, and crisps in between meals, or to watch children's videos all day... You're not an uncaring parent if you don't give them what you don't want to give them.

Q: Any advice for parents who are struggling with this issue?

A: If parents do give in, they shouldn't feel guilty about it. You know, it's easy for granny to say, 'Oh look at that mother giving that child a bar of chocolate' when you're out shopping. But when you've had tantrums in every single shop you've gone into, you may make the decision to give in at the last moment.

Q: Having experienced the same problems, do you feel a greater rapport with parents who consult you about their autistic child?

A: Absolutely, and I think the big thing I help people with is not to feel guilty if they don't want to try out certain things, because there is so much guilt in this world of special needs...what you should be doing and shouldn't be doing, and this is the therapy, and that's the therapy, but at the end of the day this may not be a battle that parents want to tackle yet, or even ever. I think it's important that professionals help to support parents in their choice because, ultimately, they are the ones going home with that child and if they decide 'I don't want to do this yet', I feel I have no right to say 'you have to.'

Q: How would you sum up your role?

A: My job is to give parents advice, support and encouragement if they want to try out various things, but if they don't I have no desire to magnify their guilt or scaremonger them. This isn't an exact science. We're all still learning about it. I always try to be very sympathetic with people.

Q: So parents are really the experts in your view?

A: Yes, I only see a snapshot of their child...I'm an expert on my son, but each parent is an expert on their child and I always allow for that. The first thing I say to the parent is, 'What do you think the problem is, what's your gut feeling?' Then I ask, 'Do you want to be here, do you want to be getting any advice?' The person who's living with that child 24 hours a day has more knowledge of the problem and a gut feel of what's going on within that child and what will work with them than any professional.

Q: What can you offer them?

A: When I advise parents of autistic children I use bits of everything...it's a combination of my own experience, what I've read and what I've been trained to do with regard to faddy eaters. It's really what works with the individual – and what works with one child might not work with another. More than anything else I listen to the parents and respect their views.

Q: Is your son's diet much improved now?

A: Oh yes. Yesterday he had his tea early and then my husband sat down to a vegetable risotto and he said, 'Can I try some of that?' A year ago that would just have been unheard of. He had two or three mouthfuls and said, 'Well, I don't really like it'. But the important thing is that he asked to try something which looked definitely adult and grown-up and unknown.

Q: What areas are still difficult?

A: He still doesn't like an extensive range of fruit and vegetables, but then again many non-autistic children are the same, so I'm not really concerned about that. He has enough of a range now for me not to worry about balancing his diet at all.

Q: Is it possible to make vegetables appealing?

A: My big breakthrough with vegetables has been puréeing soups, so he gets his quota that way. I make them very mild, so they haven't got a strong flavour, and add a little bit of cauliflower, a little bit of cream, etc. They're quite sweet-tasting and are one of my standard meals.

Q: Were there many setbacks along the way?

A: Yes, this certainly hasn't been 'abracadabra, oh my goodness isn't he eating a wide range of foods'. This has taken years. And even though he may have refused food, I still presented it to him, and I still presented it, and I still presented it. Persistence is the key and not to go in with the expectation that 'he won't eat that, so there's no point in trying.' You have to really believe that he is going to eat it and it may be that you have to offer something 100 times, and it'll be the 101st time that it's a success.

Q: Was he happy to sit with the family for meals?

A: No. He wouldn't sit at the table for more than five seconds, then he'd be up and wandering around. Sometimes he'd walk around with food. I did the classic thing that I'm sure everybody does. Once he was sat down he was given a lot of praise and attention to encourage him, but if he chose to wander off I'd ignore it. Anything to do with mealtimes – sitting down, eating, sampling new foods – was always met with loads of positive feedback, whereas not eating, saying 'I don't want that' or wandering around was simply ignored.

Q: Did you try the standard behavioural technique of giving him small amounts of new foods mixed in with something he liked, then gradually increasing the amount?

A: I couldn't do that because he would always know it was there. Even if I put a tiny amount in he could tell. I read recently that when a child doesn't like food it's almost like putting a slug on their plate. You can put that slug in chocolate but to them it's still a slug.

Q: What about reward strategies?

A: I've tried them occasionally but generally avoid them because they give the message of good food and bad food. Some people use food as a reward all the time, 'eat the dinner and you'll have the pudding' that sort of thing. The only time I used food as a reward was when I was potty training…but I try not to use it now. Food is food.

Q: What comfort can you offer parents when children are on a very restricted diet?

A: I suppose what I would say is that we are all still learning. That even though a child may appear on paper to have the most terrible nutritionally imbalanced diet, that if they are growing, full of energy and we can find a vitamin supplement they can take I would advise parents to try not to worry about their restrictive diets too much. I would however recommend that if in doubt they should try and seek professional support with a qualified dietician. First stop is their GP. A lot of children go through periods of food refusal whether or no they have special needs.

Q: Do you think eating intolerances improve generally over time?

A: I do think it gets easier as they get older, and I think part of it is that autistic and AS children develop better cognitive skills and better receptive language over the years. On the whole, although it's a broadly sweeping statement, I think the worst ages are between two and five. And that applies to normal children too. It's true that some people carry on being faddy eaters for the rest of their lives and survive quite well on it, but I think the majority improve.

Q: What is the way forward?

A: I think there needs to be some sort of multi-disciplinary approach to helping this complex group of kids. In an ideal world I'd love every parent who has an ASD child who is an extremely fussy eater to have access to a dietician, speech therapist, OT [occupational therapist], psychologist, maybe a play therapist to give parents a whole package of care. Wouldn't that be great!

13

Great Ormond Street Hospital

Jelly on the plate,
Jelly on the plate
Wibble wobble,
Wibble wobble
Jelly on the plate
(Reprinted by permission of PDF on behalf of Michael Rosen)

Great Ormond Street, one of the most respected children's hospitals in the world, has been looking after youngsters with health problems for the past 150 years. Based in central London, it is perhaps most famous for its links with Peter Pan, being funded in part by royalties from J. M. Barrie's classic play.

When it first opened, back in 1852, Great Ormond Street offered just ten beds. Today it treats some 22,000 inpatients and 78,000 outpatients annually. As part of a wide range of healthcare services, the hospital has a specialist team for children with feeding problems, including those who are selective eaters. Catherine Dendy is the clinical psychologist responsible for managing that team. At present Dr Dendy is only able to see cases that are referred from within the hospital, so the chances of your child being treated by her team are, unfortunately, quite remote. Nevertheless, she is happy to share some of the techniques and strategies that she and her colleagues have found helpful. Although she occasionally sees older children, most of the patients who attend her clinic are under the age of seven. While few of them have been diagnosed as being on the autistic spectrum, the techniques employed are still relevant:

> What we get is a lot of children who appear to be on the autistic spectrum, either because they are very small and have not yet received a diagnosis, or because they have some other problem which looks very like autism, for example, semantic pragmatic disorder. So we deal with many children who have information processing problems and therefore are uncomfortable with newness and change, and that of course also applies to food.
>
> Let me first say what we do with a standard selective eater who doesn't have those problems and then explain how we adapt that approach for children on the autistic spectrum. With selective eaters we are dealing with children who have difficulty with change and who may have had some sort of aversive experience like choking. They actually have a fear of putting things in their mouth. They may also be very texture aversive and can't be messy. They can't touch, say, sand and water, or get involved in other messy play that you typically find in a playroom or nursery.
>
> What happens is they get into a sort of battle with parents, and by the time they come to us their parents have very often given up the battle. The child will be taking just three or four preferred foods and actually thriving on these. But they are stuck because every time their parents offer them something new, they kick up such a fuss that it's not worth it. So what we do is try and work with the parents and children.
>
> We have a big playroom where the children are introduced to different textures in a very gradual way. Our play specialist has lots of different things that she does with them such as handling food and cooking. When I say cooking, I mean they are preparing things like sandwiches or putting fruit onto a kebab skewer, or making Angel Delight or whipping something up.
>
> There are also various different mixtures that the play therapist will work with – like crushed up Weetabix or cereals combined with jelly – and she'll use these to make a landscape, say, a beach with some water. At this stage they are just learning

to play with the textures, using the foods as toys. She is very inventive, so they get used to looking at these different mixtures, smelling them, touching them and being able to tolerate them on their hands.

One of the mixtures she uses consists of Weetabix, Cadbury's Flake and hot milk. This is very good for the children because they start with the Weetabix, which is very dry and flaky, and then add the chocolate which is also dry and flaky, but which melts on their hands.

There's an opportunity to say, 'Oh you've got chocolate on your fingers. Just lick it off.' Then you pour in the hot milk and start stirring, and it goes from wet to dry-wet and then into a putty kind of texture. You then roll it out and make it into a solid biscuit thing which you cut up.

The child will be there with her, one to one, and they'll be having lots of fun. Sometimes the children will start exploring the food for themselves, but they are being put under no pressure to actually do it. It's just a game.

Dr Dendy suggests this kind of approach can also be employed by parents at home, as a means of getting their children used to being close to food, touching it and even smelling it, without feeling under any obligation to eat it. In this way the child gradually learns to be comfortable around food and perhaps even starts to associate it with fun. Bringing the child into contact with certain non-food substances, she believes, can also be helpful, if it encourages them to overcome their resistance to getting their hands and face messy.

The therapist also invites the children to play with soap bubbles. If you blow them through flannel they come out in great columns. When you touch them, they burst leaving your hands feeling a bit sticky. If the children get slightly bothered by that, she'll say, 'It's OK, we can wash our hands afterwards.' But you don't wash your hands during play.

She also uses hand and foot painting, so they are learning to tolerate different textures and feelings. The idea is that once they learn to tolerate these textures on their hands, they will start to be able to tolerate them on their cheeks, on their face, around their lips and eventually in their mouths.

The Great Ormond Street feeding team tend to see children fortnightly over a period of about six months. Each visit lasts from 10 am to 1 pm. While the child is with the play specialist, the parents talk about how to manage their eating difficulties with a therapist like Dr Dendy and they also have an opportunity to observe what their offspring are getting up to in the playroom. This first part of the appointment lasts about two hours. Then, at 12, everyone comes together for lunch. The parents will be joined by their children, the play specialist and the therapist for a special meal.

> At this meal we will have a specific goal for the child. Typically with selective eaters we will start by giving them food which is very similar in texture and every other way to food they already prefer. So, if you have a child who is just eating biscuits, you introduce a different brand of biscuit. In other words, you make progress by taking very small steps.
>
> Hopefully, the child will have done some play with different biscuit textures in the playroom. Then when they come to the table we will ask them – depending on their developmental age – to touch a little crumb of a new biscuit. Then we'll say, 'Now just put it in your mouth, and eat it' and then they can have their preferred food. So they always get a reward and we always make the goal for them one which we feel they can attain.

Catherine Dendy points out that the children who come to her clinic tend to be very unsure of themselves and lacking in confidence, so it is important to give them lots of encouragement, especially when they succeed in achieving one of their goals. Parents too can feel overwhelmed by the problems they face, so she and her colleagues also use these sessions to give them as much support and advice as they can.

At the end of the session, the family is sent away with a task they feel hopeful of accomplishing during the following two weeks. Then, a fortnight later, they return and the feeding team reviews the progress

that has been made and, if appropriate, encourages the child to take
another step forward.

> So that's the straightforward case, where the child is a selective
> eater, but not autistic. Now let's turn to selective eaters who are
> on the autistic spectrum. When we come to dealing with these
> children we sometimes don't even see them on the programme
> – depending on their level of ability and their degree of diffi-
> culty. That's because the child in question may not be able to
> cope with meeting new people. The activity and noise that
> occurs in the playroom may mean it is not a conducive place for
> them to feel safe and comfortable and to learn.
>
> For these children we have a different approach. What we
> do is work with their parents on the phone, having first seen
> their child or talked about their child with them. Our assess-
> ment procedure is quite thorough. We take details of their
> medical history and their food history. We also try to video the
> parents having lunch with them.
>
> With children on the autistic spectrum you may not be able
> to make a great difference at first, but sometimes when they
> begin to talk and reason about things, you can start to employ
> the sorts of techniques you would use in any situation with
> them. Much of the time these children are highly anxious and
> need a lot of safety behaviours which are usually quite ritual-
> ised. For instance, if your child is very keen on something like
> Thomas the Tank Engine, you might sit with them and say,
> 'Every time you take a new mouthful, we are going to say
> another character from Thomas.' You use whatever they
> request. It's their safety behaviour – the thing that makes them
> feel comfortable.
>
> We also encourage them to do things like test the food out
> first, by looking at it, then by smelling it, then by touching a
> tiny bit of it and then by bringing it up to their face and just
> touching it with their lips. With children who are aversive to
> texture we do this ever so gently and reward them at every
> stage.
>
> I must stress that for children on the autistic spectrum the
> sensory part of food is very important. Great aversion can be

created by forcing a child to experience food sensations in any way and great gentleness and tact need to be used in this approach.

Those who know the child best will know how far to push them. Never, never force the child. Their world overloads them with unprocessable information and too much will lead them to 'turn off' in defence, or have a tantrum, or take avoidance action in some other way. This needs to be respected.

Something else we tend to do with children who come to see us is to give them what we call an Eat-Up book. This is a very visual thing, especially with the younger ones. What we do is get a big scrapbook and put details of foods that they are touching or just taking a tiny crumb of in the back of it. We would either cut out the label of the food or we'd get them to draw a picture of it and stick it in the book. As soon as they start taking the food in bigger amounts we would move the label or picture to the front of the book.

This then becomes their record of what they can eat and they can look back at it and show everyone what they have managed to do. They can feel very proud of the book and when they bring it in to show us what they have achieved, we give them stickers as rewards. We work very much on rewarding children.

The Eat-Up book can be helpful in other ways too. You sometimes get a pattern with children who are autistic where they apparently succeed at something and then it all stops. They may have been eating certain foods and suddenly they won't any more. At the moment that is still quite baffling to us, especially with children who are unable to talk about it or to explain themselves in any way. When this happens it can be very difficult, but as long as they are getting enough nutrients – even if they are only eating three things – you can sometimes say to parents, Well, we're just going to have to wait with this, and go back to square one.

That's sometimes where the Eat-Up book is so useful. Say, in six months' time, when the child starts coming round again to trying different sorts of foods, you can get out the Eat-Up book and ask them, 'Do you remember when you used to eat this?' So it can serve as a helpful reminder.

When setbacks like this occur, Catherine Dendy advises parents to be patient. It may be that while the child is making no progress with food, they are starting to do well elsewhere. Perhaps they have learned something new at school. Parents may have to wait while the child assimilates this new information, before they are ready to move forward again on the eating front. Dr Dendy admits that with some selective eaters who are autistic progress can be very slow or even non-existent, but her team has had some notable successes:

> We had one little boy on the autistic spectrum who wouldn't go near a certain colour of food. He didn't even like seeing other people eat food of that colour. So when he came to us and we were having lunch, we deliberately gave his mother, who was sitting next to him, some food of that colour to see what his reaction would be, and to see if we could work with that reaction. At first he was a little wary about it, looking at his mother's plate out of the corner of his eye, but actually he was then OK.
>
> Then we took it a step further by giving him some pudding of that colour. He looked at it, then reached out and touched it in a very tentative way, before picking up a spoon and trying some of it. What I think was going on was that it was a new situation for him. He wasn't at home where he expected things to be a certain way and he was old enough and not so far along the autistic spectrum to be able to cope with some newness. By introducing him to the colour he disliked we had challenged him, and we had done it when he was away from home, so he had accepted that this is what happens in a new place.
>
> In this case, I think that his parents – for perfectly understandable reasons – had become very accepting of his preferences and were not challenging him enough. In fact he moved on very well from there and actually generalised from his experience with us to start trying food of that colour at home. But it is important to remember that what we did was led by the child

himself. He was presented with an opportunity, but not pushed. We just happened to hit the right time.

Dr Dendy feels that when the boy went home he was able to accept the food colouring he had previously avoided by making a rule in his head. She believes his rule would have been along the lines of: 'Sometimes you don't like things. Then, when you get a little older, you try them again and you find that you do.' Many children on the autistic spectrum are amenable to rules of this kind. By offering them a logical path to follow, you give them a way of adjusting to new experiences. She believes that a lot of children in this situation find a rule of this kind very reassuring, because it clarifies exactly what is going to happen next.

> With the younger ones we say, 'These are the rules for trying out new foods. First of all you look.' So they look at the food and you say, 'Well done, you get a sticker for that.'
>
> Then you say, for example, if it's a jelly, 'Move the plate to make the jelly wobble', and you praise them and reward them again, and so it continues. Next you get them to place a finger on the food, then to smell it, and then to touch it to their lips. All this might take place in one session, if the child can manage it. But if it can't, we just say, 'OK, that's a little difficult for you at the moment. Maybe next time you'll be able to do it.' Then sometimes these children go away and they may say to their parents, as they are coming in on the train, 'This time I'm going to wobble the jelly.'
>
> So it's all about getting to know the child and seeing how much they can take, and working with them on a very individual basis. You have to link into their thinking, understand how their minds work and what has meaning for them. And if they are into rules and into keeping to rules, then you can really use that.
>
> Another thing that can happen is that out of the blue they can form ideas of their own about food, perhaps related to something they are obsessed with such as Thomas the Tank Engine or dinosaurs. One child I was dealing with suddenly

started wanting to eat greens, having completely refused them before. The reason was that he had seen a video of a dinosaur eating the leaves of a tree. He had decided this was greens and because he loved dinosaurs so much he thought he would eat them as well.

Another aspect of autistic spectrum disorders is the motor difficulties that people can experience. This can cause problems with the development of the mouth and jaw muscles and the ability to process more difficult textures in the mouth. Care should be taken to ensure that children can manage these textures safely. Particular difficulty may occur with chewing. A specialist speech and language therapist in feeding will be able to give exercises.

Consulting closely with parents is a key part of the programme that Catherine Dendy runs. She endeavours to discover as much as possible about the child, including how they are managing at school and whether or not they are already using a particular system, such as Lovaas. Her aim is to try to fit in with whatever strategies the child is currently familiar with.

One of the strategies is to persevere with the child and just keep presenting them with particular foods over a series of months. It may be that you give them an apple, chop it up and put it in front of them, and they won't go near it. But you just keep presenting and presenting it, without applying undue pressure on them to eat it, until they become more used to it and eventually reach out for it, and maybe explore it for themselves. So it's a question of sticking at something for a very long time, sometimes with apparently no response.

Of course, it is a very distressing situation for your child to refuse food, but I would say there is some hope. It tends to get easier when your child gets slightly older and can use their own reasoning. What you need to do is link into your child's reasoning and work with that. That's not an easy task, but it can be done. Another thing I say to parents is, if their child is getting all the nutrients they need from their particular selection of food, they can let themselves off the hook for a while and attend to other things. Perhaps they are making progress in another area, so you can say 'cool it with the food for the moment.'

Having an autistic child who is a selective eater can present parents with problems that may seem insurmountable, but despite these difficulties Dr Dendy believes there are grounds for optimism. Of course, there is no magic formula that will provide an instant cure for autistic selective eaters. But over a period of time, it's possible for real progress to be made using the kind of strategies outlined above. What helps is perseverance, sensitivity, a bit of ingenuity and, above all, patience.

There is also an eating disorders unit at St George's Hospital in south-west London. This service is available to both inpatients, and outpatients and the unit caters for those aged from 7 up to 70. Referrals are generally made through the patient's GP, but the hospital also has service level agreements with health authorities throughout the country, which means that children from all parts of Britain may be seen by the unit. The children's unit is headed by Dr Pippa Hugo, who works with a multidisciplinary team which helps to tailor individual programmes to meet a wide range of eating disorders.

14

Back to School

Pease porridge hot,
Pease porridge cold,
Pease porridge in the pot
Nine days old
(*circa* 1797)

When our children are of school age, their eating problems have a wider audience. School staff may have to take on our role and ensure that they are eating enough to keep them going throughout the day. Some schools have an enviable track record in getting children who eat very little at home to sample new foods during term time. I spoke to two head teachers who have had a great deal of success with introducing new foods on a very gradual basis.

Janet Dunn has been head teacher at John Horniman School in West Sussex for 12 years. The school is a non-maintained, residential special school belonging to the voluntary organisation I.CAN which administers three schools on behalf of local educational authorities around the country. I.CAN is the national educational charity for children with speech and language difficulties. Children from further afield, for example, Scotland, Cornwall and the north of England, attend the school as boarders, while those who live locally have the option of being day pupils. All the children have statements, with speech and language impairment as a primary disability, but some children also appear to have elements of ASD. In the current intake of pupils, aged from 5 to 11,around a third have problems with eating.

Initial assessment

The first step is to establish the extent of the problem, as the severity will determine which remedial methods are appropriate.

> School staff do a pre-entry assessment, which is quite rigorous, and at that assessment would take a case history from the family. One of the questions concerns dietary restrictions and eating problems. The staff may already be aware of the problem, as it may have been noted in the paperwork drawn up by the LEA. If it seems very severe, a decision would be made as to whether the child needed individual programming at meal-times, with one-to-one support. Where the problem is less severe, staff are made aware of the difficulty and monitor it closely, but there may not be the need for such intensive treatment. In the one-to-one situation, the child remains in the main dining room but a key worker is allocated to sit alongside them at lunchtime. Ideally, it would be the same member of staff each time, but this isn't always possible.

Monitoring the problem

The school draws up a record of progress and keeps in close touch with parents so that they can carry out the same programme when the children are at home:

> There is a core of people around the child at mealtimes and they fill in forms for each meal to record what the menu was, how the child responded to the food and how staff handled the situation. From that a handling regime is built up which all staff will follow, whether it's just one or five staff members working with the child. The keyworker team are responsible for reviewing the programmes and then alerting other staff involved.

Feeding strategies

One of the standard ways of coping with eating disorders is to introduce very small amounts of new foods to get children acclimatised to fresh tastes and textures. Some children offer considerable resistance to trying anything new, but persistence seems to be the key to success.

> Our strategy is very clear, all the children must try a little bit of everything and if they really dislike it, they can quickly move on, but they must try a little. Our menu is wide, for example, there may be sweet 'n' sour pork, or curry, and all pupils must try a tiny portion. It might be that they'll only be asked to try one pea, one very small portion of potato and one tiny piece of meat, but that is progress for a child who comes to the school eating, for example, only Sainsbury's chips, McDonald's sausages and yogurt with no fruit lumps in it. Staff might decide that simply putting the food to their lips is the first step for the child, then that's their task done. The next step would be letting their tongue stroke the food and the task is finished. Then placing the food in their mouth and finally accepting the food – without attempting to spit it out – and swallowing it. We then work on gradually building up the amount of the portion. This may be a very slow process, for example, one pea, then two, then a teaspoonful, next a dessertspoonful, and so on to a full portion.

Building motivation

Role models and peer pressure may be enough to encourage some reluctant eaters to finish food. Other children need more tangible rewards. The form this takes may vary from pupil to pupil, but the school often uses a preferred food as an enticement to try the new one.

> There is a very clear message given from the other children in the dining room who are enjoying their food. It's pointed out, 'Look, so and so is eating, and so and so has finished.' If further encouragement is needed, we'll use something that the family say is a motivator as a bribe. This may be food, but staff use whatever brings about positive results. The important thing is

immediacy. You need to sit with the child and offer, for example, a pea with one hand, while the other hand is holding the bribe, so when he or she is attempting to eat, the temptation of the bribe is right there in full view, and the reward swift to follow successful eating.

Involving parents

Ideally, parents would be implementing the same food programme at home, but this can be a very difficult requirement. As noted earlier, ASD children may compartmentalise their eating and food that is happily accepted in one setting may be rejected out of hand in another. It takes a very tenacious parent to keep serving up food that is habitually left on the plate, but the ultimate aim is to achieve consistency in the home and school environment.

> School staff talk a lot to families and let them know exactly what they are doing, and why. Parents are given a record of foods that are being successfully eaten and ones which are not. It can be very hard for families to replicate what the school is doing because home is a dynamic environment and it's not always easy to have a rigorous and consistent approach here. It may take a long time to start and finish the battle and make sure you've won. Logistically, practically and emotionally, it can be really, really hard for a family to carry out the programmes.

Table manners

For reasons best known to themselves, many ASD children have a marked preference for using fingers rather than cutlery. While this habit is excusable in very young children, it becomes increasingly difficult to justify as our offspring grow. As with all negative traits, the longer they are allowed to continue, the more difficult they can be to break.

> Many of the school's children have a preference for using fingers, because it's a lot easier. This can be a problem in the early stages, but the staff have very clear expectations and the children understand these. From day one, children are required

to use a knife and fork. It might be a special set with moulded handles or grips, but we expect children to hold them even if they don't use them properly initially. They are asked to place the implements in both hands, just to get into the habit of holding them.

Health concerns

A number of parents and health professionals have commented on the fact that although the children in their care eat a very restricted diet, they often don't appear to show any of the textbook signs of malnourishment. Some children may appear small for their years, but the majority seem to enjoy robust health and to have bags of energy – peculiarities which can make initial diagnosis very difficult. A number of the parents I've spoken to have remarked on this phenomenon: 'despite all the problems, he is extremely healthy, he went through last winter without so much as a cold'; and 'he is healthier on the whole than his elder brother, who has a completely normal diet'. Some went so far as to speculate that these children have a different immune system or metabolism to the rest of the population, managing to get exactly what they need for survival from their eccentric diets. The jury is still out on that one.

> It's often commented on how restricted the diet is and yet how the child doesn't seem to be suffering healthwise. Possibly what the child is eating at home, in the evenings or at weekends, may provide the answer to that. The family are sometimes anxious about saying what the child has eaten at home because they may be giving in to their preferred choice and might feel a bit guilty about that. The staff always reassure them if this is the case.

Success rating

At John Horniman, boarders are typically more successful at broadening their diet than day pupils, but whatever their status the battle can be a lengthy one.

Day children only have one meal a day at the school, and it may be slower progress if the family can't follow through the rigour of the programmes at home. Frequently, they find it really impossible to do. The school usually makes good progress with all children, but it can be a struggle, especially with a day child. Often families find the programme too distressing to implement. Our children are very bright and they know that kicking, screaming and throwing things around is a way to get parents to give in to their demands. Many parents will give their child whatever he or she will eat, because at least they're eating something. Thus a precedent has sometimes been set in a family that the school does not adopt, and so we start with a clean slate. Consistency is the key. If a child receives mixed messages, the problem is much more difficult to deal with. Parents may ask for children to have a packed lunch, but the school is clear on its policy and doesn't accept packed lunches. Our aim is to broaden the children's diet as much as possible.

Wider implications

Imagine the luxury of being able to take your child out for a meal or on holiday without the predictable battles we've all had to face. When the going gets tough, the school reminds families how much easier life would be if everyone in the family could appreciate the same food.

Families are asked how their children's restricted eating patterns are affecting them. Are mealtimes stressful? Can you go out anywhere with your family? Can you go out for a meal other than one that's directly dictated by your special needs child? Can you socialise? Can you go out to friends and family without taking another meal? Can your child go to parties or to a friend's for tea? What knock-on effect is all this having on other family members? Often answers to these questions give a family fresh motivation to become involved. We regularly tell parents, 'The programmes work. We've done it with other children. We know it can work.'

Words of encouragement

In an ideal world, the transition from faddy to normal eater would be a smooth and easy one that could be accomplished very quickly, without any failures or reversals. In reality, it can be a very difficult process that may be slow to show results.

> The school carries on with the programmes because the success rate is good. In some cases, children come to us eating just half a dozen foods in total and they leave us two or three years later eating a complete range of foods and a full portion. In sum, it's often a short-term battle for a long-term gain, but it can be quite a battle!

The school's ethos

Eating difficulties aren't considered as a peripheral problem at the school, but are given a great deal of consideration and weight. Speech and language therapists and occupational therapists also give input where required.

> The school has an eating skills programme in the dining room for all our children and mealtimes are as much a time for educational input as, for example, maths or English lessons, or speech and language therapy. Mouth and lip control is monitored in dyspraxic children; cutlery and plate control is important for children with co-ordination problems, etc. We have specialist therapists who use techniques to desensitise around the lips and the tongue, but mealtimes are seen as a desensitising programme in themselves. Families need to understand that if the child doesn't take the food in, the phobia will never be broken. Children have to take foods in and get used to a new feel, a new flavour. The taking of a tiny portion is the start to desensitising, it's a big part of that process.

Realistic timescales

It's the old 'how long is a piece of string?' argument. Some children may latch on to new eating programmes fairly quickly. Others will dig their heels in and may make the whole process very stressful for everyone concerned. It may take months or even years to establish a new eating regime, depending on the individual child, and the extent to which families can realistically be expected to replicate the school's techniques at home.

> The longer the habit has been in place, the worse it is. For a child at five, there's less habit, less set routine to deal with. A child at seven is much harder to turn around, and the child at nine would be even harder to change. Ideally, families would receive advice and guidance when the phobia started.

I also spoke to Kathy Cranmer, head teacher at Doucecroft School in Colchester, Essex, which caters for a number of children on the autistic spectrum with eating intolerances.

Q: Have you encountered many children who have a very limited diet?

A: Yes, when they first join us. I've worked here for over 20 years and have seen quite a number of children who, for whatever reason, have limited their own diet. Usually when we talk to parents prior to the child starting with us, their priority is for their child to eat a wider range of foods, and so we make that one of our priorities.

Q: What strategies have you found to be successful?

A: We talk a lot with parents beforehand and try to ascertain how it has evolved that the child is eating quite a limited range of food. Parents are usually very honest. Sometimes they feel it has been through some fault of their own, to some extent. For instance, when children eat very little, parents are happy to find something that they will eat and tend to provide them with that, either at a mealtime or frequent snacks between meals. It's often deemed to be more important that they eat something rather than nothing, so the choice becomes limited. Often by the time we come to have our discussion, the child is receiving a very limited diet.

Q: Do you get much resistance to trying new foods?

A: Sometimes, yes. Our school philosophy is that we do expect children to at least try everything initially, unless there is a medical reason why they shouldn't. It may be the tiniest amount of food but at least they should have a taste.

Q: How do you achieve this?

A: We formulate an individual programme for each child, which can be consistent at school and at home. The programmes vary a lot from one child to another. We usually try to include the child's favourite food, the thing they eat most often or choose to eat, in their menu. Then, gradually, we introduce little bits of other food and expect them to taste it. When they do, they get lots of praise, rewards and reinforcement.

Q: Is it a slow process?

A: It may take quite a long time. We might perhaps start off with just one different food, which might be a food that they used to eat and for some reason don't eat any more. Then we monitor the situation, record any progress, set up charts to keep accurate records. Parents are involved in that as well. However, with other children progress can be seen quite quickly. If the expectations are in place from the day the child begins at the school, these may be more acceptable as part of the whole new school environment. Some children cope better with a number of major changes occurring at the same time, rather than the gradual introduction of change.

Q: Are some cases much harder to solve than others?

A: It depends a bit on how long the problem has been going on for, how deeply entrenched it is. By and large, the more established the difficulty is, the harder it is to modify. If it has been quite a recent issue, it tends to take weeks rather than months to resolve, but with some older children, for whom it has become quite a way of life, it may well take longer. It's very difficult to generalise because sometimes when a child comes into a completely new setting like ours, perhaps the expectations are different right from the word go.

Q: Do you think children may be more willing to try things in a new environment?

A: Yes, in the past we have set up some quite elaborate programmes for children, anticipating that this would be a problem and in fact it hasn't been. So we've just presented them with what's already on the menu, what everybody else is eating at that mealtime, and they go along with it.

Q: Why do you think children may be more picky eaters at home?

A: Given all the other difficulties that children with autism and their families experience, sometimes being a picky eater isn't seen as a major issue, and parents may inadvertently reinforce obsessional mealtime behaviour or pickiness through providing the child with what he or she likes, or is known to eat. Over the weeks and months this may lead to the child only eating certain foods, or tending to refuse certain foods (based on previous experience).

Q: Do you ever feel parents aren't trying hard enough?

A: I think they sometimes don't know what to do. They feel they've tried things but maybe they haven't persevered for long enough. I think it's always helpful if there's somebody else supporting you, sharing the problem, and communicating, liaising and reviewing things with you. Maybe sometimes you have to take a step backwards, or a step forward or whatever, but you must work together and offer support in the knowledge that it will work because it hasn't failed yet.

Q: Not even with the most difficult cases?

A: Never. No, and I've been here for over 20 years now.

Q: Why do you think you succeed where others may fail?

A: We provide the children with very clear and reasonable expectations. We're not necessarily going to have them eating a roast dinner and clearing their plate from the word go, that would be somewhat unrealistic. As with most tasks, we break things down into small stages and give lots of praise, for example, for having a clean plate. It may be that there was only a small amount on there to begin with, which can gradually be built up. Consistency plays an important role too, and working with the parents. We all have to be working together. Parents have to be quite comfortable with the programme.

Q: Are parents generally happy to go along with what you're doing?

A: Yes. We are setting priorities with the parents from the word go. They often find themselves preparing a completely different menu for one child in the family and would like the child to eat with the family, trying the same food as everyone else. Once the child starts accepting more foods, we invite parents to come into the school to actually be part of the programme, so the child understands that mum or dad know that they eat this at school as well as at home. It crosses the boundaries, hopefully, between school and home.

Q: What do you typically use as a reward for eating?

A: Often the reward is food, something we know they like. It varies a lot. Some children respond extremely well to praise, others may opt for an activity they like. For some, the mere fact that it's playtime after dinner is seen as a reward as far as they're concerned!

Q: Is there a difference in the way classically autistic and AS children respond?

A: Sometimes it is more effective to involve the child with AS in the negotiations over food, because by and large they have the language skills to be able to explain why they feel they shouldn't eat, or don't eat. Sometimes it may be misguided perceptions on their part that has led to them excluding one food or a range of foods from their diet. If you can deal with those misconceptions, it may help. For example, people with AS are usually quite aware of what's going on in the world and they might respond to things like the BSE scare or salmonella outbreaks by rejecting foods. Things may get blown out of proportion in their minds and they may not fully understand the situation. Sometimes if we can work on the causes, they will more readily accept these foods back into their diet. Children with autism often respond to written or pictorial guidance about what they are expected to eat or not eat. For example, pictures of the foods they should eat made available to them, perhaps with pictures of foods they genuinely dislike with an X through them.

Q: Do you have a personal theory as to why these children can't or won't eat?

A: Some children with autism are very dependent on repetition and sameness. If they have the same meal each day, it's predictable, they know what's coming. Maybe they feel safer, more comfortable with that. To some extent, like all of us, there's slight resistance to trying different things. However, we aim to help children make decisions based on experience; therefore, you don't know if you like something or not until you've tried it.

Q: Are many children influenced by the colour of food?

A: I knew one child who had a particular liking for the colour yellow and would eat any food of that colour. He would eat other things as well but things like bananas, sweetcorn and pineapple were great favourites with him. It wasn't a problem because he wasn't excluding other colours, but he definitely had a particular liking for yellow things. We didn't make an issue of it, it was more of an observation on our part. Sometimes their likes and dislikes seem to be based on things that we wouldn't necessarily base our likes and dislikes on. The texture of food is another thing that can be very important.

Q: Have you any advice on food presentation?

A: Many children like to see their food as separate things. Sometimes I think it's tempting to try and mix food together, say, perhaps when parents are trying to disguise what's in there, but some children do not cope with mixtures very well. They like to see the peas in one place and the mashed potato in another. If a child chooses to eat all the meat first and then all the potatoes and all the peas, to actually eat them separately, I don't think that's a problem. I think quite a few people do that.

Q: Do you cope with eating problems in a low-key fashion, or is it brought out in the open?

A: It's quite low key, although we do try to make our expectations clear to the child.

Q: Have you ever used coercive tactics if children won't eat?

A: We very much work with the positive, rather than the negative. Reinforcement and praise are all important.

Q: Do you use any strategies you've evolved yourself?

A: I think it's developed over the years. We've had to work with a lot of different children with different problems at mealtimes so we've formed a basis of experience that we can draw upon to develop individual programmes with individual children.

Kathy Cranmer belongs to a group called Confederation of Service Providers for People with Autism (CoSPPA) and has helped to produce a series of booklets to assist parents with various problems including eating and drinking. The series is entitled *Working with Autism, Learning To...* and also covers a range of topics including toileting skills, sleeping problems, learning to dress, learning to play and learning to live as a family. More information is available from CoSSPA (see address list at the end of this book).

15

All Food is Good Food

There was an old man of Tobago,
Who lived on rice, gruel, and sago;
Till, much to his bliss,
His physician said this –
To a leg, sir, of mutton you may go.
(*circa* 1822)

Having children with eating intolerances wouldn't rankle so much if they had a preference for healthy foods. When your child eats, say, only four foods, it would be nice if you could announce that those four were fresh vegetables, fresh fruit, brown rice and wholemeal bread. In reality, their staple diet is more likely to consist of French fries, chopped and reformulated chicken pieces coated in batter or breadcrumbs, chocolate biscuits and bucketloads of juice sweetened with aspartame.

As parents, we know these foods appear to have little to recommend them, but we're faced with a very difficult dilemma. If we come over heavy-handed and ban these 'bad' foods, will our children willingly accept healthier alternatives? Those of you who think the answer is yes obviously haven't read the rest of the book. In the long term we should all be aiming to steer our children towards healthier and more balanced diets, but in the short term there seems little point in making a distinction between good and bad foods. If so-called bad foods are providing our children with essential nutrients and, baldly stated, keeping them alive, how can they be considered in a negative light?

Do as nanny says

I get a bit hot under the collar when guidelines are brought in, ostensibly to help our children, but which take no account of individual food foibles. A lot of attention has recently been given to the content of school dinners and what constitutes a healthy diet. At one point it looked as though chips might be banned from school menus altogether but, thankfully, common sense prevailed. However, there were reports in the media that staff were being encouraged to monitor the contents of lunchboxes in a bid to cut down on the consumption of 'unhealthy' items like crisps and chocolate. Similarly, some schools clamp down on children who bring in fruit squashes in the belief that water is a much healthier alternative. But what about the children who refuse water? Before bringing in any sweeping changes, it makes sense to consider those who can't follow these guidelines, for whatever reason. They may be in the minority, but their voices still need to be heard.

New government guidelines for school dinners in England came into effect on 2 April 2001. The recommendations were brought in to minimise health problems in school children and to reduce the incidence of eating disorders in youngsters. Legislation states that caterers should provide food including the following on a regular basis: fresh fruit and vegetables, foods high in protein including fish and meat, items containing starch such as potatoes, rice and pasta and a selection of cheese and yogurt products. These foods are depicted in pictorial form in a guide called *The Balance of Good Health* (Health Education Authority 2001).

However, items with high levels of fat and sugar such as chips, crisps and chocolate were to be restricted. All very laudable in theory, but again, the preferences of minority groups appear to have been ignored. We'd all love our children to consume healthier foods, but it's debatable whether they should be bludgeoned into doing so by restricting the availability of so-called 'unhealthy foods'. Far from reducing the incidence of problems related to eating disorders, it could be argued that actions such as these could serve to compound them.

Saving graces

Just as no foods can be written off as wholly bad, it should be remembered that the so-called good guys might not be so fantastic. A diet of fresh fruit and vegetables may be excellent, but unless you can afford the organic stuff, we may well be encouraging our kids to consume large amounts of pesticides and preservatives. But this isn't the place to get into that argument. All the foods itemised below have been classified as junk food by the population at large, but each of them also has a saving grace.

Chocolate

Apart from its 'feel good factor', some experts believe chocolate may help to reduce the risk of heart disease and strokes. Experts in nutrition at the University of California believe that polyphenols, found in cocoa, may help to lessen the risk of blood clots. Dark chocolate bars, which are low in sugar and fat, are thought to be the most beneficial.

Moreover, researchers at Osaka University in Japan think that chocolate can even prevent tooth decay (tell that to my dentist). Researchers at Osaka University discovered that chemicals present in the cocoa bean could stop harmful bacteria from damaging teeth. However, the presence of high levels of fat and sugar in most chocolate bars is definitely not good news.

If you still need convincing of its merits, chocolate provides good levels of calcium (especially the milk variety), copper, iron, magnesium and phosphorus. It also contains tryptophan which is said to increase serotonin levels, which in turn makes us feel less stressed and happy. Moreover, although cocoa butter contains saturated fats, it apparently won't increase cholesterol levels.

Chicken nuggets

Universally loved by kids but slated by nutritionists, chicken nuggets have some good points too. True they're usually made from chopped up bits of meat held together with a paste of starch and water and may have added salt, ascorbic acid and other goodies thrown in for good measure, but they're not all bad. If your child likes these, he or she will be getting a good source of protein and a helping of essential B vitamins too. However, it makes sense to read all the ingredients and try to avoid the ones containing hydrogenated vegetable oils – of course, I'm assuming that the healthier versions will find favour with your picky eater.

French fries

The oven-baked variety of chips will always score points over the fried variety, containing just 5g of fat per 100g portion, but fries aren't all bad. In general, the thinner the fries, the more calories and fat content they'll contain, as they soak up more oil than their chunkier counter-points when cooking. Where possible, try to steer your kid's interests towards the thicker variety. French fries are also a good source of vitamin C. While we're on the subject of potatoes, broadly, it's worth remembering that these are a good source of fibre and contain high doses of vitamin C and the mineral potassium.

White bread

If you give your children the choice of a wholemeal loaf or a pasty white one resembling cotton wool, chances are they'll opt for the latter – if they can make up their minds, of course. However, white bread isn't all bad. Nowadays, goodies such as vitamin B1, calcium, iron and niacin are added to the flour to make it more nutritious and white bread is also low in fat.

Pizza to go

If you avoid the big breakfast variety, pizzas can be quite healthy. Most ASD children I spoke to seemed to prefer the plainer varieties, with simple toppings of tomato and cheese. Cheese is a good source of protein, calcium and conjugated linoleic acid (CLA), which is believed to stop arteries from clogging up. If you're making your own pizza, canned tomatoes are a good source of lypocene, which is thought to help cut down on heart disease and cancer. Tomatoes also contain potassium and the vitamins, A, C and E. If they'll experiment with flavours other than cheese and tomato, steer them towards relatively healthy chicken or vegetable versions.

Fatty foods

Don't dismiss all fats – children need a diet that's relatively high in fats as they're growing. Ideally we should all avoid a diet that's high in saturated fats, but those found in foods like pilchards and mackerel are the good guys, as are the mono-unsaturated sort contained in olive oil and avocados. If your children like cheese, they'll also be taking in lots of the good fatty acid CLA.

Epilogue

If this were a fairy story, the ending would be a happy one and I'd be able to reveal that my child no longer had eating intolerances and was enjoying nutritious and balanced meals. In reality, he's taken a few steps backwards and is at the stage of minutely dissecting every piece of breakfast cereal in an abortive search for 'bits', which means that very little gets eaten. I'm quite au fait with what to do in theory now, but am fully aware that putting these guidelines into practice is far from easy. In general, Harry's diet is much better than it was a few years ago and I'm proud of all the progress he's made, but there's still a long way to go. For those of us who feel cheated if we're deprived of a happy ending, the following observations might help to redress the balance a little:

Reasons to be cheerful

- You don't have to waste your money on fancy Cordon Bleu cooking courses, because to your child bland will always be best.

- Our children's heightened sensitivity to taste and smell will decrease as they get older. We all start off with around 10,000 taste buds but these mercifully die off as we age. By age 70, it's estimated that we'll have lost around one-third to a half of them. If this loss occurs at an even rate, we all stand to lose around 50 to 70 taste buds a year.

- If food and restaurants become one of their obsessions, you're in luck.

- Be grateful that your child is reluctant to put foreign substances in his/her mouth. It dramatically decreases the likelihood that they will grow up to be drug abusers, alcoholics, smokers or members of Weightwatchers in later years.

Okay, I'll pose for the picture, but don't expect me to eat the stuff

Bibliography

Attwood, T. (1998) *Asperger's Syndrome, A Guide for Parents and Professionals.* London: Jessica Kingsley Publishers.

Batchelor, J. and Kerslake, A. (1990) *Failure to Find Failure to Thrive.* London: Whiting and Birch.

Bryant-Waugh, R. and Lask, B. (1999) *Eating Disorders: A Parent's Guide.* London: Penguin.

Gerland, G. (1997) *A Real Person, Life on the Outside.* London: Souvenir Press.

Green, C. (1984) *Toddler Taming: A Parents' Guide to the First Four Years.* London: Century Hutchinson.

Hall, K. (2001) *Asperger Syndrome, the Universe and Everything.* London: Jessica Kingsley Publishers.

Health Education Authority (2001) *The Balance of Good Health.* London: The Stationery Office.

Kedesdy, J. H. and Budd, K. S. (1998) *Childhood Feeding Disorders.* Baltimore, MD: Paul H Brookes.

Kessler, D. B. and Dawson, P. (1999) *Failure to Thrive and Pediatric Undernutrition.* Baltimore MD: Paul H Brookes.

Lewis, L. (1998) *Special Diets for Special Kids.* Arlington TX: Future Horizons.

Opie, I. and P. (1951) *The Oxford Dictionary of Nursery Rhymes.* Oxford: Oxford University Press.

Pearce, J. (1991) *Food, Too Faddy? Too Fat?* London: Thorsons.

The Principals Group, National Autistic Society and Local Autistic Societies (1991) *Managing Feeding Difficulties in Children with Autism.* London: National Autistic Society.

Rosen, M. and Steele, S. (1993) *Inky Pinky Ponky.* London: PictureLions.

Schaal, B. (2001) 'Acquired Taste.' *New Scientist 169* 2272, 13.

Siegal, B. (1996) *The World of the Autistic Child.* Oxford: Oxford University Press.

Stanway, A. and P. (1988) *The Baby & Child Book.* London: Peerage Books.

Wing, L. (1987) 'Feeding Problems in Autism.' *Communication, 21,* 7–9.

Further reading

Green, C. (2000) *Beyond Toddlerdom.* London: Vermilion.

Holliday Willey, L. (1999) *Pretending to be Normal.* London: Jessica Kingsley Publishers.

Underdown, A. (2000) *When Feeding Fails.* London: The Children's Society.

Useful Addresses

Confederation of Service Providers for People with Autism (CoSPPA)
7 Bevan Drive
Alva
Falkirk FK12 5PD
Scotland
Tel/Fax: 01259 769768

Doucecroft School
163 High Street
Kelvedon
Colchester
Essex CO5 9JA
Tel/Fax: 01376 570060

Feeding Team
Great Ormond Street Hospital
London WC1N 3JH
Tel: 020 7405 9200

John Horniman School
2 Park Road
Worthing
West Sussex BN11 2AS
Tel: 01903 200317

LDA
Duke Street
Wisbech
Cambs PE13 2AE
Tel: 01945 463441
Write for a Primary and Special Needs catalogue.

National Autistic Society
393 City Road
London EC1V 1NE
Tel: 020 7833 2299

Special Needs and Parents (Snap)
Keys Hall
Eagle Way
Warley
Brentwood
Essex CM13 3BP
Tel: 01277 211300

A support group for parents and carers of children with any special needs or disability.

Spectrum
St Giles Centre
Broomhouse Crescent
Edinburgh EH11 3UB
Tel: 0131 443 0304

Early educational support for children with autism and related communication needs. Programmes incorporate TEACCH methods.

St George's Eating Disorder Service
Harewood House, Springfield University Hospital
Glenburnie Rd
London SW17 7DJ
Tel: 020 8682 6747

Websites

Association of the British Pharmaceutical Industry.
www.emc.vhn.net

British Dietetic Association
www.bda.uk.com

British Homeopathic Dental Organisation
www.bhda.org

Bureau for Information on Tooth Erosion
www.bite.uk.com

Dietitians Unlimited
www.dietitiansunlimited.co.uk

Holistic Dentistry
www.positivehealth.com

National Autistic Society
www.oneworld.org/autism_uk/index.html

Additional thanks must go to:

Jennifer and Christina, Helga and Aidan, Heather and Jonathan, Karen, Nathan and Daniel, Linda and William, Chris and Maxwell, Janet and Paul, Anne and John, Sarah and Thomas, Alison and Samuel, Ann and Dylan, Mark and Jack, Linda and Patrick, Grace, Lisa and Nicholas, Sharon and Darren, Justine and Samantha, Julie and Andrew, Jackie and Adam, Matthew, Karen and Jack, Glynis, James, Matthew and Paul, Donna and Jack, Paul and Carl, Linda and Hywel, Maureen and Thomas, Antonia and Harry, Rosalyn and Charlie, Catherine and Robert, Benjamin, Peter and Charlie, Maggie and Thomas, Dee and Leon, Cathy and Matthew, Catherine and John, Angela and Joe, Karen and Daniel, Diane and Russell, Rosalind and Philip, Sharon and Joe, Clare and Jackson, Brenda and Emma, Gaynor, Robert and Richard.

Index